Civil War II

THE COMING BREAKUP OF AMERICA

by
Thomas W. Chittum

American Eagle Publications, Inc.
Post Office Box 1507
Show Low, AZ 85901
—1996—

3 4 5 6 7 8 9 10 11 12 13 14 15

Library of Congres Cataloging-in-publication data:

Chittum, Thomas W., 1947-
  Civil War II : the coming breakup of America / by Thomas W. Chittum.
    p. cm.
  Includes index.
  ISBN 0-929408-17-9 (alk. paper)
  1. Political violence—United States—Forecasting. 2. Militia movements—United States—Forecasting. 3. Social conflict—United States—Forecasting. 4. United States—Social conditions—1980-
  I. Title.
  HN90.V5C49 1996
  306'.0973—dc21   96-48938
                                                       CIP

Contents

CIVIL WAR TWO

America:
Empire or Nation?

"History is littered with wars which everybody knew would never happen."—Enoch Powell, Member of the British Parliament

America was born in blood. America suckled on blood. America gorged on blood and grew into a giant, and America will drown in blood. This is the spectre that is haunting America, the spectre of Civil War II, a second civil war that will shatter America into several new ethnically-based nations. Many will denounce this truth as racist and as a call to violence. It is neither. Rather, it is the result of an objective examination of the historic, demographic, political, economic, and military developments that are relentlessly propelling America towards a second civil war. Simply and directly put, America will explode in tribal warfare in our lifetime and shatter into several new ethnically-based nations. And as America breaks up the very concept of multiethnic democracy will likewise be forever shattered. Artillery will blast our cities to flaming wastelands infested with psychotic snipers. Packs of feral dogs will tear at charred corpses hanging out of burnt-out tanks. Long columns of doomed refugees will clog our highways. Bands of guerrillas will stalk about the countryside—raping, looting, murdering, clashing with each other. Food production will all but cease. The hungry will fight to the death over scraps of garbage. Millions will starve, and millions more will die from infectious diseases. Behold the vision of Civil War II.

The underlying cause of this second civil war is nothing less than the very nature of our country and its peoples. There are, essentially, two types of geopolitical entities—empires and nations—and they're best considered by contrasting each to the other.

Empires are generally larger, sometimes even global in scope, and more likely to be geographically fragmented. Nations, on the other hand, are usually smaller and geographically continuous.

Empires consist of peoples of different religions, languages, cultures, races, and nationalities. One of these groups, a minority itself, dominates the others by naked military power. Nations, on the other hand, are dominated by one group that makes up a majority of the population. Finally, and most important, nations are inherently stable while empires are always inherently unstable. Nations are naturally stable because a majority of the people mutually recognize each other as co-nationals. Multiethnic empires never achieve true internal stability. They survive only by unrelenting military and police suppression of their inhabitants, and break up the minute the dominant group loses the military power, or the will, to shackle the empire's peoples together.

To understand the future, study the past. Throughout world history, all multiethnic empires have broken up, and almost always in cataclysmic violence. Therefore, the question is not if the multiethnic American Empire will shatter, but when and under what circumstances.

The former Soviet Union and the former Yugoslavia are classic examples of multiethnic empires that recently shattered in tribal violence. The Russians had historically been the majority ethnic group in the former Soviet Union. However, the percentage of Moslems had been steadily increasing while the percentage of ethnic Russians had been steadily falling and had sunk to about 50% in the mid 1980s. The old Soviet Union did not long survive the decline of its dominant ethnic group, and neither will America. Actually, the Russian Empire is still with us, just renamed and shrunk down to a more nation-like, and therefore more stable, demographic base. (Russia is now about 80% ethnic Russians.) Clearly,

America is a hybrid displaying both empire-like and nation-like characteristics. America is empire-like in its immense size, its geographic fragmentation, and its great diversity of races, religions, language groups, nationalities, and cultures. America is nation-like only in that it is still dominated by the English-speaking Europeans, the group that's been the majority in this country since its beginning in revolutionary violence. It is instructive to recall that America was born in revolutionary violence because the British establishment was treating us as second-class citizens to be exploited in their multiethnic empire.

Now, ongoing and dramatic changes in this country's ethnic composition are rapidly transforming America into a more empire-like entity, a naturally unstable political card-house doomed to collapse exactly as every other multiethnic empire throughout world history. Projections by the Census Bureau indicate that by approximately 2050 AD, less than sixty years from now, nonwhites will become the majority in America, and Europeans a minority. The current (1992) figures are: Whites 74.8% Blacks 11.9% Hispanics 9.5% Asians 3.1% Indians 0.7%. The projections for 2050 AD are: Whites 52.5% Blacks 14.4% Hispanics 22.5% Asians 9.7% Indians 0.9% (See Figure 1).

How fast is America being transformed? In the 1960s America was about 89% white, then a liberalization of the immigration laws caused a surge in the nonwhite population. Since the Sixties the white percentage of the population has fallen at about the rate of 1/2 a percentage point every year. It is clear from the census projections that the government expects (and is actually causing) this process to continue at about the same or an increased rate.

Another way to highlight the demographic transformation of America is to consider an America without any increase or decrease in the total population. In this illustrative case, a daily decrease of about 3,000 white people would be offset by a daily increase of about 3,000 nonwhite people. At this rate America would also be reduced to about 50% white by

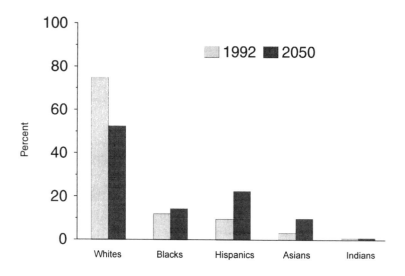

Fig. 1a: Population of the United States, Percent.

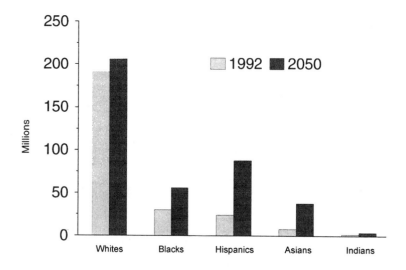

Fig. 1b: Absolute population of the United States.

the middle of the next century. That's how rapidly America is being transformed. It's as if every day 3,000 whites were disappearing and being replaced by 3,000 minorities. Every single day! This is a sort of statistical ethnic cleansing engineered through liberal immigration laws and unchecked illegal immigration.

It's time to start thinking the unthinkable. When Civil War II fractures the multiethnic American Empire, what military patterns will the conflict take on as events unfold? What new nations will emerge, and where will their boundaries be based on current ethnic patterns and the military resources of these new nations? And what signs will measure our inevitable slide into all-out ethnic warfare?

It must be kept firmly in mind that there is nothing critical about any particular date or set of percentages. Many other factors will also affect the rate of our downward spiral into ethnic warfare and the partitioning of the multiethnic American Empire by Civil War II. Key events should be closely monitored and dispassionately analyzed. Consider the following events and decide for yourself if America is proceeding towards a second civil war or not. . . .

Trends in American Riots

Urban riots have long been a fact of American life, and many were ethnic in nature. Today, they are almost exclusively ethnic in nature, and it doesn't take much to ignite one. Electrical blackouts, unpopular legal decisions, traffic accidents, real and imagined police brutality, and racial incidents of all sorts are commonly followed by ethnic riots. Urban riots have preceded almost every revolution and civil war in western civilization since the Industrial Revolution, and they are now preceding Civil War II in America. If you disagree, consider these trends in rioting:

Trend 1: Heavy Weapons

Watch future riots to see if heavy weapons such as attack aircraft, artillery, or armored vehicles are used to suppress them. If they are, we'll know we've taken another critical step towards Civil War II. Actually, in the Los Angels riot of '92, armored personnel carriers were used by the Los Angeles police to flush out organized snipers in the predominately black Jordan Downs housing project.[1] Armored personnel carriers are not police vehicles; armored personnel carriers are military attack vehicles. Armored vehicles were necessary because the riot was not actually a riot, but a hybrid somewhere between a riot and a war. It is a stark fact that these riots are increasingly taking on the characteristics of outright warfare, and that the police are increasingly and necessarily taking on the characteristics of armies in order to fight these wars. This ongoing conversion of our police departments into military formations is reflected by their increasing use of armored vehicles, helicopters, bullet-spraying assault rifles, combat helmets, bulletproof vests, military uniforms, sniper rifles, and military organizational structures such as SWAT teams.

Trend 2: Ethnic Militias

Watch riots for confrontations between armed ethnic militias, because such confrontations will certainly precede Civil War II. Actually, a confrontation between armed ethnic militias has already occurred. In the Los Angeles riot of '92, Korean merchants spontaneously formed a *de facto* ethnic militia.[2] They armed themselves with pistols and shotguns, stationed themselves on the roofs of the buildings in their shopping center, and coordinated their defense of their property with citizen band radios. In so doing they successfully defended their property against similar armed ethnic militias composed of black street gang members that torched much of Los Angeles. In the Los Angeles riot of '92, armed ethnic

---

1 Robert Vernon, *L.A. Justice*, Focus on the Family Publishing, 1993, pp. 22-27.
2 *Newsweek*, "The Siege of L.A.", May 11, 1992, p. 38.

militias confronted each other on American soil, but the significance was missed, intentionally or otherwise, by the politically-correct establishment media. Why?

Trend 3: Barricades

When rioters erect barricades, they're taking an important step, consciously or unconsciously, towards creating a new nation, however small or temporary. These barricades are boundaries. They proclaim that all on one side are of the same tribe, and that all on the other side are foreigners. These barricades are physical boundaries that are preceded by and reflect the boundaries in the hearts and minds of those who erected them. After these physical barricades are torn down by the police, the barricades still remain in the hearts and minds of those who erected them, and therein lies the real problem, because barricades in hearts and minds can not be torn down by any amount of police force.

Trend 4: Siege of Police Stations

Nations do not allow hostile armed forces on their territory, so watch for rioters laying siege to police stations and military installations. The media will call these sieges attempts to punish the police or capture their weapons, but that's only half the truth. The greater truth is that, consciously or unconsciously, these rioters are creating a new nation, and that they perceive the police as the occupying army of a foreign power. Also, watch for attempts to seize radio and television stations, and government buildings.

Our Unstable, Tiered Society

"The only stable state is the one in which all men are equal before the law."—Aristotle

Multiethnic empires are always tiered, undemocratic societies because it is impossible for empires to be other than tiered, undemocratic societies. Empires are always undemocratic because the diverse peoples making up the empire have nothing in common to serve as the foundation for the empire's laws—no common mythology, no common language, no common culture, no common history, and—most important—no common vision of the empire's future. Therefore, the laws of an empire are always unpopular with most of the empire's subjects, who would certainly either take over the empires's government, or set up their own new nation on a portion of the empire if they could do so democratically. Therefore, the people must be denied democracy in order to hold the empire together, and force must be used to keep the resulting undemocratic and unpopular imperial government in power.

Empires are necessarily tiered because a certain group or groups must be given special privileges to enlist their support in the subjugation of the other groups. The more groups an empire has, the more tiers it will have.

Empires have laws, of course, but they're a facade, and massed behind the facade and ever ready to smash the inevitable rebellions of the empire's subjects are the appropriate military formations—the Pretorian Guard of ancient Rome, the Royal British Navy, Hitler's Waffen SS, the KGB and

MVD internal security forces of Russia, and whatever band of mercenary thugs that will be charged with binding Imperial America together. The cynicism that always accompanies undemocratic, imperial governments promotes corruption, social tiering, militarism, racism, tribalism, and intolerance of all conceivable varieties.

Few geopolitical entities can be neatly described as entirely democratic or imperial, and most exist at some point in the spectrum between the two. Chiefly because of our ongoing demographic transformation, America is now drifting from the democratic, non-racist and nation-like end of the spectrum towards the undemocratic, racist and empire-like end of the spectrum. This ongoing transition has been accompanied by social upheaval and violence, and the future necessarily holds increasing levels of both, culminating in an all-out tribal civil war. This erosion of democracy due to our ongoing demographic transformation into an imperial state is rightly becoming the focus of separatist groups. One such group is the Southern League whose goal is secession and independence for the southern states, nothing less than a second Confederacy. Here's how two of their spokesmen, Mr. Michael Hill and Mr. Thomas Fleming, expressed their concern in an article entitled "The New Dixie Manifesto" which appeared in *The Washington Post*:[1]

> "What had been a genuinely federal union has been turned into a multicultural, continental empire, ruled from Washington by federal agencies and under the thumb of the federal judiciary. And all this is done regardless of the party or ideology that controlled the White House."

Now that America is fast evolving into an undemocratic multiethnic empire, prudent individuals will reflect upon

1 *The Washington Post*, "The New Dixie Manifesto", by Michael Hill and Thomas Flemming, October 29, 1995, Section C, p. 3. (The address of the Southern League is PO Box 40910, Tuscaloosa, AL 35404, phone (205)553-0155.)

what tier they've been assigned to by our politically-correct social engineers. Even nation-like America was a tiered society, and the top tier was always the English-speaking Europeans. They constituted the top tier because they possessed the greatest military power and were not shy about using it, and they possessed the greatest military power for several brutally simple reasons:

First: They were more numerous.
Second: They had, and kept to themselves, the economic power.
Third: They controlled the political machinery.
Fourth: They mutually recognized each other as co-nationals and considered all others second class citizens, subhumans to be enslaved, or vermin to be rid of.
Fifth: They had privately owned firearms, a final assurance that they, both as a group and as individuals, held real power and rights that even their own government would dare not tamper with lightly.

Because of these factors, the English-speaking Europeans held the military power in America, and because they held the military power, they formed the uppermost and only significant layer of American society. Now, the balance of real military power is slipping away from the (working-class) English-speaking Europeans because they're fast losing the five underlying advantages that sustained that power. Now, the tiers of our society are being rearranged to reflect their growing or eroding share of the demographic, economic, political, and, ultimately, military power. What are these tiers of the emerging multiethnic American Empire, and what tier have you been assigned to? Some are listed below. I invite you to decide for yourself.

The International Bureaucratic Elite

Somewhere near the very top are the international bureaucratic elites. Currently, there are approximately 37,000 foreigners residing in America who are literally above American law. The members of this elite can, and often do, violate American laws including acts of rape and theft without any legal consequences whatsoever. American police cannot arrest them, nor can American courts put them on trial. Currently, approximately 37,000 resident foreigners enjoy full or partial diplomatic immunity.[2] Not all are even diplomats. Some are merely servants of diplomats such as chauffeurs. The rights of American citizens have fallen so low and the privileges of the international bureaucratic elites have risen to such heights that even the servants of these international elites may freely assault American citizens without penalty. In fact, if you strike back, the police may arrest you.

Since World War II the number of foreign residents enjoying diplomatic immunity has risen dramatically, both in absolute numbers and relative to the American population. Monitor your daily newspaper for reports of crimes against American citizens committed by members of the diplomatically immune, international bureaucratic elite.

If diplomatic immunity is extended to the administrators of international organizations and treaties such as the United Nations, NAFTA and the International Monetary Fund, we shall have another clear sign that Civil War II is approaching, because it will signal that the members of the international elite are formalizing their power and taking over, and that they will not suffer any interference by American police or courts. Actually, many officials of the United Nations already enjoy diplomatic immunity. This is significant because none of these UN personnel are bona fide diplomats because they have not been sent by one sovereign nation as its representative to another sovereign nation. In theory they are merely international civil servants who have no proper claim whatsoever to traditional diplomatic immunity. In fact,

---

2 Chuck Ashman and Pamela Trescott, *Diplomatic Crime*, Acropolis Books, Ltd., 1987.

they've received diplomatic immunity because the UN is an important tool of the New World Order, which needs both an international bureaucracy immune to interference by national police forces, and an international military force sufficient to crush internal rebellions of subject nations, formerly free nations euphemistically known as member states.

Now America is being methodically transformed into a typical third-world basket case of a country, a racially and socially tiered undemocratic society exactly like the ones these third-world bureaucrats come from, so they can pillage this country exactly as they pillage their own countries. To stop the tiering that is tearing our nation apart, our constitution should be amended to absolutely forbid diplomatic immunity to anyone under any circumstances. If that causes some foreign tyrant to break diplomatic relations, then so be it.

The International Super Rich

Another top layer of the emerging American Empire is composed of the international super rich.[3,4] The American super rich are increasingly abandoning their increasingly worthless American citizenship to join the set of the international super rich. Each year, more super-rich Americans renounce their citizenship to avoid paying American taxes. Typically, they become nominal citizens of micro countries where they pay nominal taxes.

Our corrupt American politicians have arranged that these ex-American super rich can still legally reside in America for much of the year by posing as tourists. In effect, the American super rich have bribed our corrupt politicians into exempting them from any taxes whatsoever without any penalty what-

3 *Forbes Magazine*, "The New Refugees" by Robert Lenzner and Philippe Mao, November 21, 1994, p. 131.
4 *Time*, November 28, 1994, p. 96.

soever except for an extended Caribbean vacation every year.[5]

Watch to see if this new class of ex-American international super-rich turncoats continues to grow, and if they are allowed to come and go as they please. This will indicate that the members of the wealthy and corrupt American establishment are reserving this tax loophole for their future personal use, and that America is that much closer to Civil War II. If they do, then being an American will be a smear (like poor white trash) reserved for a tier of society that is sinking lower and lower in economic and political power and therefore, ultimately, military power.

English-speaking White Americans

Eventually, being an American will be meaningless in practical terms, and therefore there will be no point in the continued existence of America at all. Eventually, for working-class white Americans, our ethnic group and income level will be our *de facto* nationality.

The racist euphemism for this systematic dismantling of the rights of English-speaking Europeans is affirmative action. Increasingly, economic opportunities and even legal rights are determined not by your status of being an American citizen or not, but by your ethnic group. Increasingly, government documents require that individuals state their ethnic group. This data is not merely for informational purposes.

The politically-correct social planners have assigned English-speaking Europeans to the very bottom layer of imperial America, and racist affirmative action is the tool they're using to construct their brave new world. Even though racist affirmative action will suffer occasional setbacks, eventually this racist concept will triumph completely. Eventually,

---

5 Perhaps we need a law requiring that all wealthy Americans who have renounced their citizenship be permanently banned from reentering America under any circumstances.

the growing minorities and their New Order allies will seize absolute political power and expand racist affirmative action to all areas of everyday life in the new multiethnic American Empire. This racist concept of affirmative action is the single most important test of how close this country is to Civil War II, and it raises questions:

Question 1: What tier of the multiethnic American Empire do you think you've been assigned to?

Question 2: Do you personally think your assigned tier is rising or sinking in legal rights and economic opportunity?

Question 3: When being an American no longer means anything at all, what will you then consider your nationality to be?

These are no mere rhetorical questions. I really want you to think over these three straightforward questions until you've given yourself direct and honest answers. The politically-correct elitists who run the multiethnic American Empire keep telling middle-class, white Americans that they are now whites first and Americans second. Have the imperial elitists seriously considered what will follow when most white Americans actually start to agree with them?

Illegal Aliens

Currently, illegal aliens occupy the very bottom tier of American society. Since most are nonwhite and non-English-speaking, they currently occupy a station lower than their assigned tier in the new politically-correct, undemocratic, multiethnic American empire. Accordingly, means will be found to raise their legal status up to and over that of European, English-speaking Americans.

How will this be done? Our corrupt politicians will grant amnesty to illegal aliens so they can become citizens and receive racist affirmative action special privileges. When our corrupt politicians give amnesty to illegal aliens, it's another flashing red warning indicator that Civil War II is that much closer. Actually, our corrupt politicians have already granted amnesty to illegal aliens with the Immigration Amnesty Act of 1986.[6,7] This amnesty legalized over 3 million illegal aliens, most of them Mexicans, who are now becoming citizens after the seven year waiting period. Also, In May 1995, President Clinton allowed 20,000 Cubans to legally settle in America. These blacks and Hispanics are now eligible for racist affirmative action special privileges, which you are not if you are white, and these blacks and Hispanics will doubtless be inclined to vote for politicians who favor even more racist affirmative action programs. Also, watch to see if the establishment media drops the term illegal alien and substitutes the politically-correct euphemism, undocumented immigrant.

Watch for more such amnesty acts in the future. There are millions of illegal aliens residing in America, almost all of them nonwhite. Should they be granted citizenship, the cultural and political landscape of this nation will be radically and permanently altered beyond peaceful modification.

American Indians

American Indians are another minority being granted special privileges. They're allowed to build casinos on their reservations on the pretext that these reservations are sovereign nations not subject to American law. If these reservations are sovereign nations, why are the residents allowed to vote in American elections, and why are they allowed to receive welfare?

A group of native Hawaiians who want an independent Hawaii[8] have received multiple grants from the Federal Ad-

---

6 *The Economist*, May 20, 1995, p. 29.
7 *The New York Times*, "Amnesty for Cubans", May 21, 1995, Section I, p. 8.
8 International People's Tribunal Articles 9, 10. (Address: Tribunal

ministration of Native Americans, grants that have added up to approximately one million dollars,[9] to advance their agenda. Their post-independence agenda includes ongoing foreign aid, a century's "back-rent," and unspecified "reparations" from the US government. Non-Hawaiians should note that their agenda makes no absolute guarantee of recognizing the property rights of people who are not native Hawaiians. (If these Hawaiian secessionists would include absolute guarantees of property rights for non-Hawaiians, stop using racist terms like "red-neck," in their literature, and drop their demands for reparations and "back rent," I'd have no serious differences with them. However, that's not the posture they've chosen.)

We all know what sort of reaction white separatists get from Uncle Sam, and it never includes gratuitous million dollar checks. In the case of Randy Weaver's wife, it was a sniper's bullet in the head. When considering euphemisms such as affirmative action, diplomatic immunity and undocumented immigrants—don't think of them merely as mechanisms of convenience used to grant special privileges to minorities and strip English-speaking white Americans of their legal rights. They have a much broader, deeper, and more sinister goal that is not immediately apparent unless examined from the proper perspective—the perspective of Civil War II. That goal is nothing less than the destruction of American citizenship and therefore, ultimately, the destruction of America itself.

In multiethnic empires, the concept of citizenship does not have the same meaning of conveying rights as it is commonly understood by Americans. In the multiethnic British Empire, for example, the people were first and primarily subjects of the Crown, which decided what their rights were, based on their ethnic group and social class, not on their status

Komike, 333 Ka'ohinani Dr. Honolulu, HI 96817.)
9 *The New York Times*, November 8, 1992, National Report, p. 24..

of being a British citizen or not. In the multiethnic Soviet Union, the establishment's bureaucracy determined the rights of individuals based on their ethnic group, which was duly stamped on their identity papers, and their membership, or lack of it, in the establishment's sole political party.

Now that America is being re-engineered into an undemocratic, multiethnic empire, our concept of citizenship must be (and is being) destroyed, and is being replaced by ethnic group and social class, because the concepts of a multiethnic empire and rights based on citizenship are absolutely and completely incompatible.

Mao Tse-tung's Rules For Revolution

"Political power grows out of the barrel of a gun."—Mao Tse-tung

Many civil wars start when some group concludes it's not getting the political and economic power it should based on its military power. At that point, they use their military power to get more political and economic power, and that's the way the real world usually works. People directly relate might with right and conduct themselves accordingly. Now that America is fast becoming an unstable, multiethnic empire doomed to disintegration, where will the boundaries of the new nations be based on demographic patterns and the military potential of the various ethnic groups? Mao Tse-tung knew that political power is derived from military power, plain and simple, and the Great Helmsman knew much about real power. Mao Tse-tung, it should be recalled, led a long, bloody, and successful guerrilla campaign in China, defeating both the Imperial Japanese Army and the rival, western-supported forces. His works on the theory and practice of guerrilla warfare are closely studied at West Point, and all other military academies worldwide. Mao Tse-tung held that there are three necessary conditions for a guerrilla movement to succeed:

Condition 1 is the active support of a significant portion of the population, say 10%. It is sufficient that the remainder are apathetic or terrorized into submission.

Condition 2 is secure sanctuaries for the guerrilla formations to operate from. An adjacent country whose government actively supports the guerrillas is ideal, but in-country sanctuaries such as jungles, swamps or mountains will suffice.

Condition 3 is ongoing aid from a foreign government in the form of financial assistance, armaments, diplomatic and other support. [1]

Mao Tse-tung stated that, generally speaking, without these three conditions, guerrilla movements have historically been defeated or have devolved into bandit gangs. These last cautionary words of Mao Tse-tung should be carefully weighed by the constitutionalist militias now forming in America.

American patriots enjoyed all three of Mao Tse-tung's conditions in their struggle against the British Empire and won. The Confederacy of our first civil war lacked ongoing foreign assistance and lost. While neither of these were entirely guerilla wars, they do serve to lend credence to Mao Tse-tung's observations. There is nothing sacred or certain about Mao's three rules, but let's keep them in mind as we analyze the military potential of America's main ethnic groups in order to understand how events will unfold as each carves its own new nation out of the collapsing multiethnic American Empire.

---

1 Samuel B. Griffith, *Mao Tse-Tung on Guerrilla Warfare,*Praeger Publishers, p. 27, 28. (Originally published in 196, but this edition contains an introduction of post-Vietnam vintage.)

The Mexican Reconquista of our Southwest

"You're Mexicans—Mexicans who live north of the border."
Mexican President Ernesto Zedillo in a speech to Mexican-American politicians in Dallas, Texas in 1995[1]

In 1916,[2] in our own century, Pancho Villa and his revolutionary soldiers—or drunken banditos, take your pick—rode out of their Mexican sanctuary and into Columbus, New Mexico shouting their battle cry, *"Mata los gringos!"* (kill the gringos!). And kill the gringos they did, and they burned and they looted. Before they were driven back to Mexico by the hot pursuit of the American Army, Pancho Villa's bandito revolutionaries killed 17 Americans, both civilian and military, male and female.[3]

Today, Pancho Villa is a Mexican folk hero. Today, Mexican ethnics are the majority in much of the southwest. Long before 2050 AD, they will be the majority in all of the southwest. As the Hispanic population surges past 50%, Spanish will replace English as the dominant language. New waves of Mexican immigrants won't have to learn English to

---

1 *The New York Times,* December 10, 1995, Section B, p. 15.
2 *The New York Times,* March 10, 1916, p. 1.
3 T. R. Fehrenbach, *Fire and Blood,* Macmillan, 1973, p. 524. Charles C. Cumberland, *Mexico, The Struggle for Modernity,* Oxford University Press, 1968, p. 366.

work or collect welfare, so they won't bother to. Thus they will not be assimilated into American society as previous Mexican immigrants have been.

Demographics and affirmative action will purge the Anglos out of police departments and other branches of local government. Bilingualism will increasingly be mandatory for both government and private employment. Eventually, a working knowledge of English will not be a requirement for government employment at all. Eventually, Anglo citizens who speak only English will be hard pressed to obtain any government employment or services. The southwest will be transformed into a Spanish-speaking, *de facto* province of Mexico. Enforcement of immigration laws by Hispanic-controlled police departments will disappear entirely. Some Hispanic-controlled police departments will publicly announce their defiant refusal to enforce immigration laws. Millions of desperate, poverty-stricken Mexicans will stream across the border. The southwest will be American only in a sense best described as a legal fiction—a meaningless flag fluttering overhead and a federal army of occupation to prevent the disaffected locals from tearing it down.

If this scenario sounds farfetched, recall that it parallels how formerly Mexican Texas was settled by waves of Anglo immigrants who rebelled and set up their own nation the minute they assembled the military resources to do so. Now history is running in reverse, and the Mexicans are taking the southwest back. Like it or not, admit it or not, ignore it or not, the Mexicans are taking the southwest back, and short of sealing our border with Mexico there is precious little we can do about it. These events will not occur in isolation. Long before the middle of the next century, Mexico will experience at least one, and more probably a series of, catastrophic revolutions. The classic Mexican revolution usually features most of these signature events:

1: A Southern, Indian-based uprising which is traditionally put down by the wholesale slaughter of Indians by the

Mexican Army and Spanish-ethnic militias. The current Zapatista uprising is exactly such a rebellion.

2: A Northern uprising seeking to break the political domination and eternal corruption of the Mexico City-based, Spanish-ethnic elitist clique. The Northern-based PAN party will probably stumble into such an armed rebellion unless it is co-opted into the spoils system.

3: Initial victories by the revolutionaries as they overwhelm smaller detachments of the regular Mexican army, who will be hampered by their corrupt officers who will fight ineffectively or flee.

4: Riots in Mexico City by students, labor unions, the usual agitators, and just plain hungry people.

5: Proclamations by Mexican Army officers, police officials, or regional political leaders in favor of the central government in Mexico City, or in favor of the revolution.

6: Rebel and federal hordes laying waste to the countryside. When there is precious little left to loot, burn, rape, and murder locally, they start towards the big pinata of Mexico City. At this point, the Mexican President either makes a grand speech, loots the treasury and flees   or stands and fights. Making a stand involves importing large amounts of arms from abroad—meaning America or a European power—and reorganizing the Mexican Army.

7: If the Mexico City-based, Spanish-ethnic clique wins, then a great slaughter of Indians, and mestizo peasants takes place, and things are promptly back to normal. If the revolutionaries capture Mexico City, some bandito/revolutionary becomes president. However, since only the Spanish-ethnic, elitist clique is capable of running the country, they're always right back in power within a few years. Then the giant corruption-revolution wheel starts yet another great creaky turn. Watch for these events as Mexico topples into civil war because its waves of refugees will flood across our borders.

The coming revolution in Mexico should not be dismissed as a sort of comic fiesta of tequila-swilling banditos firing pistolas into the air to the tune of *La Cucaracha*. Mexican revolutions make ours look like frat house food fights. The last serious Mexican revolution lasted from 1910 to about 1920 and resulted in the death of from 1 to 2 million Mexicans out of a population of just over 15 million. Something like 10% of the entire population perished. The corresponding figure for our first Civil War is 2%.[4]

In the last Mexican revolution, armies of federal soldiers and revolutionaries roamed the countryside. The worst would take over a town like movie bikers, rape all women and girls who made the cut, loot everything worth stealing, and smash and burn everything else. Few objected. Those who did were lucky if they were shot. Many were castrated, hung, or variously tortured to death. A favored amusement of one Mexican general was a "fruit tree," a tree from which a dozen or more were hung simultaneously. The next Mexican revolution will likely be somewhat different due to changed circumstances. One suspects that the worst fighting may be in Mexico City itself. Certainly, vast numbers of refugees will flee across the border seeking food and the protection of American law.

The American government is preparing for exactly such a scenario. In 1995 near Nogales, Arizona the Border Patrol and the military cooperated in field testing an "Enhanced Border Control Plan."[5] Compounds of tents surrounded by chain link fences and barbed wire were constructed for the express purpose of detaining and processing anticipated massive waves of illegal Mexican immigrants. What might cause such an overwhelming inflow of illegals? According to a US government spokesman as related to a New York Times reporter the causes might be: "A natural disaster, or the

---

4 *Brother against Brother*, Time-Life Books, p. 408.
5 *The New York Times*, December 8, 1995, Section B, p. 16.

economy collapses, or the military attacks the government, or any number of other situations."

Similar exercises have recently been held elsewhere, including near McAllen, Texas.

Mexico is utterly corrupt, a swirling cesspool of corruption. Hundreds of rich Mexicans have been kidnapped for ransom in the past several years, mostly by gangs tied to drug cartels and Mexican police departments.[6] In March 1994 a Mexican police commander and two of his men were arrested when they tried to hijack a car belonging to the son of Ernesto Zedillo, the President of Mexico.[7] The moonlighting police commander, by the way, had served a prison term for murder prior to being accepted by the police.

The entire border area is a sinkhole of crime and gunfire. Gangs of Mexican banditos are looting Southern Pacific freight trains that pass near the border.[8] During a recent 18 month period, over 100 trains were looted, with the Mexicans carrying off everything from TVs to frozen fish.

Eventually, the corrupt Mexican establishment will be overthrown and replaced, most probably by leftist, gringo-baiting revolutionaries not unlike the Sandanistas of Nicaragua. Economic collapse and increasing population pressure will drive millions of Mexicans across the border where only a few will find work, and most will survive on government assistance in slums and refugee camps. These poverty-stricken illegal aliens will further aggravate the artificial labor surplus in the Southwest, driving wages down even further, accelerating the ongoing flight of working-class whites.

Multinational corporations will squash all efforts to turn this tide of events. They will continue to bribe our corrupt American politicians with PAC money. Even more NAFTA-

6 *The New York Times*, June 25, 1994, p. 6.
7 *The New York Times*, March 3, 1995, p. 7.
8 *Newsweek*, Aug. 21, 1995, p. 69. *The Economist*, June 17, 1995, p. 31.

	Percent White 1995	Percent Hispanic 1995	Year White = 50%	Year Hispanic = 50%
Arizona	68%	27%	2016	2041
California	51%	34%	1996	2036
New Mexico	46%	49%	1991	2006
Texas	57%	35%	2003	2025
All	54%	28%	1999	2031

Based on projections of US Census Bureau figures. The projections here may be realized much earlier due to incresed white flight and Hispanic immigration

Fig. 2: Border states and their demographic future.

style treaties will be put into effect, which will further impoverish working-class people in both Mexico and America, and hasten the downward spiral into Civil War II. Bitter, energetic, and unemployed young Mexican and Mexican-American males will flock to guerrilla training camps south of the Rio Grande, camps actively supported by a radical Mexican government. The reconquista will then shift into its active military phase.

The seeds of this future have already sprouted. There exists a campus-based group of Chicanos advocating an independent Hispanic nation in the American southwest, a nation they have given the name of "Aztlan."[9] You will hear more of this Aztlan in the future, because illegal immigration, tribalism, and white flight are constructing this new nation day by day, every day.

---

9 Peter Brimelow, *Alien Nation*, Random House, 1995, p. 194.

New Mexico was the first state of the union *to become a miniature third-world nation* in recent American history. It became so about 1991 when whites were no longer a majority in New Mexico. In about the year 2006, Hispanics will become the actual majority of the population of New Mexico, and it will live up to its name and become a *de facto* part of Mexico. It will be the first state to fall to the demographic reconquista, and without a single shot having been fired. The shooting may come at some future date when the Mexican flag or the Aztlan flag goes up and the tanks roll out of federal military bases as the government tries a counter reconquest. Then there will be an abundance of shooting.[10]

Today, about half the first graders in Texas are Hispanics.[11] When they reach adulthood the Hispanics will outnumber the Anglos. The long-awaited reconquista of gringo-occupied Northern Mexico has begun. *Reconquista*— that's the word the Mexicans have for their reconquest of their occupied northern territory—currently, but only temporarily, our American Southwest.

The first Reconquista occurred when Christian knights drove the Muslim Moors out of Spain, starting in the Eleventh Century AD. Now, Mexicans see this first great Reconquista as inspiration for their own recovery of their patrimony stolen by the army of blue-eyed invaders. If you can't take the Reconquista seriously, ask yourself if you would fight to regain American soil that had been conquered and occupied by foreigners.

Do you think Mexicans are any less brave or less devoted to their country? Do we think of the Texans of the Alamo as Mexican traitors or American patriots? If legal nationality

------

10 California will be the second third-world state in about 2010 when Anglos will account for less than half its population. See Robert A. Pastor and Jorge G. Castaneda, *Limits to Friendship—The United States and Mexico*, Alfred A. Knopf, Publishers, 1988, p. 293.
11 Lester A. Langley, *MexAmerica*, Crown Publisher, 1988, p. 170.

counts for more than tribal affiliation, why do we hail the Alamo defenders as American heroes rather than spit on them as Mexican traitors? Many, perhaps most, were, we should recall, naturalized Mexican citizens and/or legal immigrants. They swore an oath of citizenship and allegiance to Mexico, and they broke their pledged word. When Texas declared for independence, many Americans spontaneously rushed to Texas and the defense of their tribal brothers. Does anyone really think Mexicans will be less courageous and stay at home when their tribal brothers likewise raise their flag over Los Angeles?

In the year 1999, the southwest will cease being nation-like in its ethnic composition and became empire-like, because no single ethnic group will constitute an absolute majority. Shortly afterwards, the southwest will again become nation-like in its ethnic composition because the Hispanics will be an absolute majority. The natural and historic political cycle will be repeated, and secession will occur, certainly violent, probably to the point of all-out war. And bear in mind that Table 2 does not take into account increased illegal immigration or increased white flight out of the southwest. If you are an Anglo living in the southwest, or in fact any non-Hispanic living in the southwest, you are well advised to leave as soon as practical, certainly within the next five years.

Incredibly, the Reconquista threatens not only the southwest, but ultimately the entire nation. According to the Census Bureau, in 1994,[12]

"For the first time ever, more Hispanics were added to the U.S. population than whites."

In summation, the Hispanic guerrilla movement in the southwest will enjoy all three of Mao Tse-tung's conditions for a successful guerrilla movement: Support of the people;

---

12 *US News and World Report*, August 14, 1995, p. 9.

suitable sanctuaries to operate from, both in-country and across the Rio; and the ongoing support of a foreign government.

Open, all-out warfare will start with a wave of massive urban riots setting the southwest ablaze from Houston to San Francisco, with the epicenter in Los Angeles. Spanish-speaking police and National Guardsmen will side with the rioters, raise the Mexican flag, and lay siege to federal military installations. An outright invasion across the Rio Grande by regular Mexican Army units will likely follow.

At this point, the federal government will have only two options: surrender the southwest to Mexico, from which we originally stole it, or attempt to take it back by a massive, all-out invasion by our regular federal military, which may or may not succeed, and will certainly require the use of heavy weapons, intensive street fighting, and straight-up genocide cleansing.

Technically speaking, the future revolt in the southwest should not be thought of as Hispanic guerrillas fighting the American military on U.S. soil. Rather, it must be more accurately recognized as an invasion of northern Mexico by the American military, a task whose inherent difficulty is more readily apparent. Recall that the southwest will in reality be Mexican, and foreign invaders—by which I mean the U.S. military—will have no choice but to resort to ethnic cleansing to win, because mere occupation will result in continuous guerrilla raids against the occupiers, exactly as would be the case if the American Army crossed the Rio Grande and occupied northern Mexico today.

The Reconquista Checklist

Watch for the following developments that constitute a checklist of events that will unfold as we edge closer to the abyss of Civil War II in the southwest:

Item 1: A requirement by any local or state government that its employees must be fluent in Spanish.

Item 2: A lack of requirement by any local or state government that its employees must be fluent in English.

Item 3: The adoption of policies by school boards that Spanish classes be mandatory or that instruction in English be optional.

Item 4: The demand by a Mexican political party or a major politician that the southwest of the United States be returned to Mexican sovereignty.

Item 5: The formation of an Hispanic-based political party in America.

Item 6: The increasing display by many Mexican-Americans of nationalistic symbols such as the Mexican flag, in much the same manner that many African-Americans now commonly wear Malcolm X hats.

Item 7: The emergence of a revolutionary guerrilla movement in Mexico.

Item 8: The overthrow of the Mexican establishment, either by an election, *coup d'etat*, or revolution, that brings an ultra-nationalistic government to power, either right-wing or left-wing.

Item 9: A general economic collapse in Mexico followed by a massive surge of illegal aliens into America.

Item 10: The expansion of the Border Patrol or its conversion into a military force equipped with heavy weapons.

Item 11: The massing of American military units near the border, or the involvement of our federal military in border control.

Item 12: The massing of Mexican Army units along the border.

Item 13: The public refusal by a police department controlled by Hispanics to enforce immigration laws, for individual Hispanic policemen to refuse to enforce these laws, or for any association of Hispanic law enforcement officers to equivocate about these laws. Also watch for the first instance of an Hispanic-American law enforcement officer who can not speak English.

Item 14: Any cross-border raid by Mexican revolutionary guerrillas into America, however small. This will breach an important psychological barrier and lead to more such incursions.

Item 15: The common occurrence in America of urban riots by Mexicans or Mexican-Americans as riots by African Americans are now common.

Item 16: The formation of Hispanic militias in the southwest.

Item 17: The recognition of dual citizenship by the Mexican government for Chicanos and for Mexican immigrants who become citizens of America. The Mexican government will use this concept of dual citizenship to involve itself in internal American affairs such as promoting racist affirmative action for Hispanics, influencing American elections, and interfering in matters concerning control of our borders.

Item 18: Watch for Mexican-Americans claiming legal rights to land currently owned by Anglos, claims based on the old Spanish royal land grants. When Mexico was a colony of Spain, Spanish kings granted large tracks of land to their Spanish and Mexican subjects in what is now the American southwest. The Mexican government continued legal recognition of these grants after Mexico won its independence from Spain in 1821. After our war of aggression against Mexico, the southwest was surrendered to us by the Treaty of Guadalupe Hidalgo in 1848. Under the provisions of this treaty, the United States was to respect these land grants. We didn't. We Anglos stole most of it straightaway. As soon as the Hispanics control the legal and law enforcement machinery in the southwest, they will steal it back, straightaway, every last square foot of it, probably under color of law, but by leveled rifles if they are impatient. This cycle of land stealing illustrates as well as you please how the real world works: (A) The Spanish immigrants stole the land from the Indians by genocide. (B) The Spanish immigrants redefined themselves as Mexicans, revolted and stole the entire country from the Spanish Crown. (C) The Anglos stole the land from the Mexicans by wars of secession and aggression. (D) The Mexicans and Mexican-Americans will steal the land back, either by direct force in Civil War II, or under color of law backed by the police force of the state.

Item 19: Watch for the appearance of third-world slums in American cities. They will almost certainly appear first in the sprawling urban barrio centered in East Los Angeles, or the dismal Hispanic agricultural towns near Fresno, California, or adjacent to border towns like El Paso. They will be straight out of Mexico City, built of cinder blocks, plywood, tin and even cardboard, with illegal and dangerous pirate electrical hookups and no sewer hookups.[13] Any attempts to evict them will bring accusations of racism, and will spark riots.

Item 20: Watch for border incidents involving exchanges of gunfire between Mexican police and/or military on one side and American police and/or military on the other side. One such incident was reported in the *New York Times.* On Aug. 10, 1995, a U.S. Border Patrol officer on the American side of the border was shot in the back by one of two Mexican (Nogales City) police officers on the Mexican side, who then crossed over the border onto American soil and continued firing at the American patrolman and his partner, neither of whom fired back. According to the the *New York Times* the border is now an area of "low-level conflict,"[14] so expect an escalation of such shooting incidents in the future.

---

13 *The New York Times,* March 27, 1988, Sect. I, p. 1. *The New York Times,* Jan. 3, 1989, Sect. I, p. 12. *The New York Times,* April 2, 1995, Business Section, p. 1. *The New York Times,* June 20, 1995, Sect. D, p. 8.
14 *The New York Times,* Aug. 20, 1995, p. 5.

Item 21: Watch for a general exodus of working-class whites out of the southwest, especially the border area, and increasing mention of this flight in the establishment press. This will be accompanied by a downward spiral and even a collapse in real estate prices in the southwest.

Item 22: Watch for all manner of violent and disruptive incidents in Mexico—Derailments and looting of trains; hijacking of trucks; seizure of the Haciendas of the wealthy; massacres of peasants; mutiny in the army; occupation of factories and government offices by workers; soldiers and police firing on protesters; units of the security forces engaging each other in firefights; formation of private security armies; bank robberies and ransom kidnappings of the wealthy by revolutionaries; food riots; all manner of sabotage; show trials followed by public executions; corpses dumped along roads; a general exodus of the wealthy to Europe and America; another and even more serious collapse of the peso and a massive flight of capital; a collapse of the stock market and the economy in general; the removal of the seat of government from Mexico City; the storming of the Presidential Palace by a mob; the resignation and exile of the President; the seizure of Mexico City by a revolutionary body.

This concludes the checklist for Civil War II in the southwest. Some items of this checklist, such as the establishment of a rural guerrilla movement in Mexico, have already occurred to one degree or another. I leave it to the skeptical to check off the others, one by one.

The Mexican Establishment

Much has been made of the supposed commitment of the Mexican establishment to transform Mexico from a one party socialistic dictatorship into a capitalistic and multiparty, Western-style system. This much-touted transformation was, and continues to be, a complete and premeditated sham. The ownership of state corporations was simply transferred to the

Mexican elite—stolen, actually. In 1987 there was one Mexican billionaire, by 1994 there were 24, all from this wholesale looting of state property.[15] The Mexican elite has no intention of allowing real democracy and honest government in Mexico. They know perfectly well that they would lose any honest elections hands down, and that they would be put against the walls of their own luxurious haciendas and shot. The Mexican elite has its own clear vision of a new Mexico—a sham democracy, complete with sham elections and sham freedom of the press. The intention is to finance it by the profits from their slave labor Maequiladora factories, ongoing drug trafficking, and blackmail bailout money from our corrupt American politicians intimidated by threats of waves of illegal aliens should Mexico collapse.

The bailout isn't working, or rather it isn't working if one judges it by its avowed goal. On the other hand, it is working quite nicely when judged by its actual goal—the bailout money is going straight into the bank accounts of the Mexican elites, and their unindicted co-conspirators in the American financial establishment. The more realistic members of the Mexican elite have seen the handwriting on the wall, and are simply bailing out. The former Deputy Attorney General of Mexico, Mario Ruiz Massieu, was arrested at Newark Airport in New Jersey with $30,000 in cash in his possession. Subsequent investigation revealed he had 10 million dollars in various Mexican and American bank accounts.[16]

The former President of Mexico, Carlos Salinas, has fled Mexico for permanent exile in America and elsewhere. His brother has been arrested on suspicion of murder, and reportedly has a stolen horde of $84 million (US) dollars stashed in various Swiss bank accounts.[17] As for "subcomandante" Mar-

---

15 *The New York Post*, January 18, 1995, Patrick Buchanan's column in the Editorial Section.
16 *The New York Times*, May 10, 1995, p. 12.
17 *The New York Times*, Nov. 25, 1995, p. 4.

cos, if he is not killed or captured by the Mexican Army he will go into exile in France and be lionized by Parisian café society. Then the Indian uprising in Chiapas will get serious.

The uprising in Chiapas, by the way, was organized by old school, hard-line, Spanish-ethnic Marxists centered in Mexico city and its Autonomous Metropolitan University, the traditional nursery for middle-class, leftist revolutionaries in Mexico. Subcomandante Marcos has since skillfully usurped the leadership, purging all who stood in his way, and he now calls all the plays however much he may deny it. If not killed, he will sooner or later, probably sooner, cash in his publicity chips and head for his natural habitat, the fashionable café society of Europe with all its fawning ladies. Watch for this guy on the lecture circuit. He is a self-promoter, and he will probably desert his Indian cannon fodder to advance himself as President of post-revolutionary Mexico, because he sees the coming explosion in Mexico clearly. The revolution in Chiapas will never shift into high gear until its leadership passes to the hands of the Indians and mestizo poor. Mexico's biggest immediate problem is that the old system of the dictator/President heading the PRI Mafia with its absolute monopoly on force and corruption has broken down. Before the drug explosion, the PRI Mafia controlled all corruption and power right down to every last peso, burrito and pistola. The President was the untouchable, supreme Aztec who spoke exactly once concerning everyone's place and fate. Thus, everyone knew his place and more importantly—what would happen should he forget. Few forgot. The system was custom designed and put in place expressly to stop the great revolution of 1910 to 1920, and to prevent its reoccurrence, and it worked. It worked because the PRI elite held a jealously guarded monopoly on both money and guns. Not any more, amigos!

Enter the drug and gun mafias. They evolved in a Darwinian world where the one rule was that you shot and shot and shot until shot dead yourself. Because of the explosion in American drug consumption after the Vietnam war, especially cocaine, the gun mafias grew so rich and powerful that they corrupted the police. The police had always been totally corrupt, of course, and by design, but strictly within the pecking order set by the PRI. Assassinations of PRI and other establishment bigs were forbidden as were turf wars.

Now there is simply no longer any center to Mexican society, no supreme Aztec atop the highest pyramid in Mexico City. The gun mafias have ridden into town like Cortez, and they are not impressed with Zedillo or his effete and feathered PRI high priests. The Mexican center has not held, things are falling apart. Various local political bosses, businessmen, police chiefs, mafias, guerrillas and military commanders are amassing what amounts to private armies, many with heavy weapons. They answer only to superior force, and only if immediately and liberally applied.

Worse yet, since Mexico is now multi-centered, the old method of fine tuning the machine by occasional murder has broken down. Before the gun mafias turned Mexico into a narco-republic, when a body was found by the side of the road the appropriate people knew who did it (and usually why) because there was a monopoly on power. Nowadays, in multi-centered Mexico, it is impossible to track the assassins and assorted killers to their paymasters. It's all a horrid version of "Who's on First," and not even President Zedillo himself can be sure who is assassinating whom or why - a 180 degree, destabilizing reversal of the old system. To be sure, the old system was horrid, but it was a system that did prevent the greater horror that it was designed to prevent—the ultimate, mega- horror of civil war.

Watch for more assassinations and other signs of the collapse of the traditional Mexican system and its elite, and watch for signs of what will replace it, because the hyenas have started to devour each other.

Revolution in the Black South

"I am not an American; I am one of twenty-two million black people who are victims of Americanism." Malcolm X

Today, Malcolm X, not Martin Luther King, is the historic voice of young blacks. What of southern blacks and their military potential? The unfolding of events in the southwest is clear, at least in the final result. In the south however, events will be dictated as much by external forces as internal ones. The black population of the south is growing faster than the white population, partially because of the higher black birthrate, and because blacks of the northern cities are increasingly returning to their southern home states because crime has turned the northern black slums into concrete killing fields.

This trend of blacks returning to the south should continue as third-world immigrants, particularly Hispanics, have taken much low-skilled employment that is the primary source of black income in northern cities.[1] In addition, immigrant third-world entrepreneurs, who provide much urban employment these days, often hold violently racist attitudes about blacks. Blacks should remind themselves that many third-world immigrants are entirely without the sense of historic guilt that many northern whites embrace. Depending on how strong and how long these demographic currents flow, the south will either tip into a black majority / white minority posture before

---

1 *The New York Times*, "Liberals Duck Immigration Debate" by Michael Lind, Sept. 7, 1995, p. 27.

Civil War II erupts or it will not. It is manifest to objective observers that serious ethnic warfare to the point of secession will first erupt in the southwest, with Los Angeles being a good bet for its epicenter. After the Mexican reconquista of the southwest, all will realize that America as a multiethnic nation is psychodelic fiction from the '60s, and ethnic conflict will flash across the south. Depending on many factors, but primarily the demographic factor, two scenarios are likely. We shall first deal with the black majority / white minority scenario.

The Black Majority / White Minority Scenario

By 2050 AD, blacks will certainly be the majority in the states of the deep south. The southern black establishment will seize political control, first of the major cities, exactly as they've already done in Atlanta, Georgia. The whites will flee to *de facto* white enclaves, exactly as they're now abandoning Atlanta, seeking refuge in Forsyth and Dawson Counties to the north of Atlanta.

The wealthy whites of the old southern establishment— seeking to retain their power and property—are spouting much nonsense about power sharing and a supposed new south. It is a pathetic exercise in self-deception. As in the southwest, demographics and racist affirmative action will force out the whites, starting with the non-property owning, working-class whites.

To the victors go the spoils, and the new black establishment will gorge itself. Their loot will come from increased taxes that will intentionally bankrupt and drive out white business owners—from municipal contracts from which white businessmen will be barred by racist affirmative action—from kickbacks and corruption of all sorts—from protection payoffs from black gangs grown into mafias, and from stolen federal aid meant for the poverty-stricken citizens of their cities.

These cities controlled by the black establishment will be one party mini states, and therefore utterly and irreversibly corrupt. The power base of the black establishment is the slums of poor, bitter, and radical blacks. And the black establishment will prudently see to it that their power base remains poor, bitter and radical. White flight will accelerate, and blacks will become the voting majority in one southern state after another. The black establishment will then legally seize entire state governments in elections, one after another, precipitating even more white flight.

The actual sequence of military conflict in the South will be complicated by two factors. One is the number and size of the remaining white enclaves. The whites of these enclaves will increasingly become radicalized and form self-defense militias. Clashes with black militias and black-controlled police forces will occur, and they will steadily increase in frequency, duration and violence until most white enclaves are abandoned or overrun. Only those white enclaves on the periphery of the black heartland have any real chance of long-term survival.

Another complicating factor will be alignment of the northern-dominated federal government, which at first will support the powerful black establishment because of its vote-delivering power, but will quite possibly be seized by revolutionaries of one type or another at some point. As in the southwest, the federal government will face the dilemma of massive and indiscriminate use of heavy weapons against its own citizens, or acquiescing to southern black independence.

Civil War II in the south will be widespread due to the close intermingling of the races, which the white flight into enclaves will only partly reduce. It will also be utterly without mercy due to the mutual hatred and loathing so deeply rooted in southern history. Unlike the Mexican aliens in the Southwest, all blacks are citizens who can vote, and they have a cohesive establishment that is already seizing power legally and gradually, thus skipping the guerrilla stage of Civil War II, at least initially. In fact, the first guerrilla and/or terrorist formations to appear in the south will almost certainly be white. Military virtues, traditional values, patriotism, religious fundamentalism, adherence to cultural norms, and distrust of central authority have long been features of southern white culture. Likewise, many white Southerners tend react to events in a very personal and immediate manner, a characteristic that confounds Yankees. All these are characteristics of a warrior culture, not unlike Afghans or Apaches, and this southern white warrior culture will have much impact on the unfolding of Civil War II in the south.[2]

The south has been an occupied country since Civil War I, or at least psychologically occupied, and the threat of federal intervention was the only thing that kept the south from all-out tribal warfare in the sixties. Should the threat of federal intervention fade for any reason, genocidal warfare could erupt in the south. The whites and blacks in the south exist in a state similar to the Tutsis and Hutus in Rwanda. They are intermingled, they are in economic, political and psychological competition, and they have no mutual history except that of mutual loathing and hatred.

Blacks are seizing political power in the south, and white southerners face the stark reality that guerrilla warfare will be their only realistic reply to legally constituted black political/military pressure in the form of black politicians and black police who will combine to abuse whites, seize their property under color of law, and generally make life untenable. And all this will be done with the cooperation of the federal government, the federal police, the federal judiciary, and the federal military.

In summation, the course of events in the south will likely follow this scenario:

1: The blacks will seize political power legally, at least in the deep south.

---

2 *The New York Times*, "Better at Fighting, by John Keegan, Feb. 24, 1995, Literary Supplement, p. 3.

2: Whites will flee to enclaves within the south, and many will abandon the south altogether.

3: The corrupt black establishment will utterly impoverish the areas under its control, possibly leading to a takeover by revolutionary black extremists.

4: Fighting will erupt between the blacks and the militias of the remaining white enclaves, in which most of the whites will be killed off unless rescued by the federal government.

5: The final result will be an independent black nation in the deep south, with Atlanta its probable capital.

Mao's rules for protracted, rural-based revolution don't apply well in the south, because the blacks will acquire power legally, and because the whites have the option of fleeing. Rather, events in the south will more likely follow the Yugoslav model, where massive fighting broke out almost overnight following a total breakdown of central authority.

This breakdown of authority might take the form of the overthrow of the black establishment by black radicals, or an attempt by the federal government to reassert its authority, or by spontaneous outbursts of genocide of whites by blacks, and blacks by whites. In any case, casualties will be massive as remaining white enclaves within the new black nation are overrun and black enclaves in white territory just outside the boundaries of the new black nation are likewise eliminated.

The White Majority / Black Minority Scenario

What if the blacks are not the majority in the south when Civil War II begins in earnest? They will lose, to be sure, but what will they lose and what will they be left with? In this black minority scenario, events will unfold much as in the black majority scenario, but they will seize no more than, say, three state governments prior to Civil War II, perhaps none. Instead of surrounded white enclaves, surrounded black enclaves will fall to ethnic cleansing. It is still probable that the whites will allow the blacks a homeland—the Mississippi

Valley as far north as Memphis and scattered pockets of the "Black Belt" as far north as Washington D.C..

The other possibility in the event of white victory is the assigning of the blacks to another category entirely consistent with the western concept of total war. This alternative is soul-chilling, but we must not shy away because Civil War II may topple us into this abyss. To understand this possibility, we must digress a bit and rethink our concept of war. . . .

> *"War is the continuation of politics by other means."* Carl von Clausewitz, Prussian general and western military philosopher.

The ghost of Carl von Clausewitz[3] still haunts the nightmares of professional soldiers and statesmen alike because no moral man among them has yet made a reply to his implied axiom, or even admitted openly what the Prussian dared to hint at. The Prussian aristocrat forever struck the concept of war from the moral constellation where his predecessors had placed it. If he had falsely proclaimed that war was ennobling, he would have gone down in history with lesser men such as Nietzsche. If he had condemned war as immoral, he would have been dismissed out of hand. In his book, *Vom Kriege (On War)*, Clausewitz stated that wars are affairs to benefit the "state," an entity expressed as a sort of secular trinity of the establishment, the people, and the military - that this "state" had interests that were sometimes most conveniently expedited by the "other means" of war, and sometimes not. Clausewitz reduced war to the dispassionate status of a sort of carpenter's tool, nothing more, to be applied when expedient to the extent sufficient. No longer would statesmen and generals have to fuss with God, ethics, morals, honor, and similar pre-industrial, pre-Darwinian bores when making the decision to initiate war. Men were now at once the both measure of all things, and the object of their own quantification. Darwin, von

---

3 Carl von Clausewitz, *On War*, Penguin Books, 1982.

Clausewitz, and Adam Smith—the authors of the apocalyptic era, an era about to climax.

But what measures sufficiency? What indeed? Clausewitz held that "War therefore is an act of violence intended to compel our opponents to fulfil our will." But Clausewitz made no direct mention of the temporal dimension of will, or of the cyclical nature of political will-fulfilling that yoked all Europe to endless circling around the mill of war as if Europe were a mindless ox. The answer lies in Clausewitz's Prussian concept of honor that compelled him to state, "War is nothing but a duel on a larger scale."

Ironically, the Marxists were students of Clausewitz, and endorsed his technical concept of war, which fit Marxist constructions quite nicely. Their consideration of the temporal dimension was the establishment of a global communist society that was to be permanent—the last and final revolution. After the Marxist revolution, there would simply be no more wars, as wars were nothing more than the inevitable clashes between competing cliques of capitalists.

Hitler also studied Clausewitz and, because he was a true revolutionary, grasped Clausewitz's error when he said: "Generals think war should be waged like the tourneys of the Middle Ages. I have no use for knights; I need revolutionaries." There you have it. No honor, no duels, no knights, but a completion of the revolution that the aristocrat started. Not only did Hitler separate the decision to wage war and morality, he also separated its conduct and morality. More importantly, he considered the meaning of will and the temporal dimension.

Hitler's answer to the temporal problem was also a permanent order in which opponents strong enough to challenge Germany would simply no longer exist, not even potentially. Hitler conceived to relieve Germany forever of the endless cycle of war by the direct extension of Clausewitz's logic upon selected categories of Germany's perceived internal and external antagonists. Hitler's deficiencies were moral and practical. He was guilty of no inconsistency between his philosophy and its application, and his military philosophy was straight von Clausewitz, no chaser.

The scenario of Clausewitzian total war in America is not inevitable, but must be considered without flinching: Contrast the situation of the blacks to that of the Hispanics. There are something on the order of 90 million Mexicans in Mexico, and perhaps another 25 million Hispanics in America. They are a formidable military force. Moreover, there are numerous Spanish-speaking countries whose opinions matter to a degree of caution. African-Americans, on the other hand, are far less numerous and have not nearly so powerful a foreign constituency.

Who would actually commit themselves to the military defense of American blacks? Who would actually regret their passing beyond a brief spasm of chest beating sufficient for the usual ceremonial hypocrisy? If this attitude seems objective to the point of *realpolitik*, observe that it will reflect the real attitude of many at the time of Civil War II. And reality, after all, not currently fashionable platitudes or mythology, is our focus of analysis. Blacks should prepare themselves for such an eventuality. They would be well advised to make restricting Hispanic immigration their next-to-primary strategic objective. They should reflect on how blacks are universally abused in Hispanic countries. Current America will go Hispanic, but blacks can prepare for such an eventuality. The more time passes, the more they are likely to take demographic and military possession of the old South. Time is on their side, and the later Civil War II erupts, the more likely they will secure their indispensable sanctuary.

Their medium term strategic interests dictate an accommodation to white interests, however bitter this reality is. Their northern black ghettos are, and will continue to be for some time, militarily vulnerable. Their southern sanctuary is still not secured, and is at present hardly a string of sub-regional enclaves. Premature ignition of Civil War II could well mean a solution imposed upon blacks by whites who will grasp the principle of total war intuitively, if not directly and intellectually.

Note that Hitler was a student of Clausewitz, a student who surpassed his master, and brought his philosophy to its resolution. The measures that Hitler took were consistent with total war and our currently accepted western philosophy of war as originally expressed by Clausewitz. To those who say that Hitler was a psychopath, it must be noted that they are entirely correct. But they must also understand that his psychopathic reasoning was entirely consistent with our current western, Clausewitzian philosophy of war, and with the social conditions of imperial societies, including our own imperial America, which are similarly rooted in the psychopathic axiom that people are best judged by some social engineering cocktail of tribe, social class, and the crimes of their ancestors. In imperial America, our current version of this psychopathic axiom is racist affirmative action. As America becomes more imperialistic, we shall also become more psychopathic along group lines. Sooner or later, we will topple into civil war. When we do, we will embark on a program of systematic punishment of groups deemed responsible for this or that misfortune, just as happened in Nazi Germany. You cannot adopt a system of government without receiving to a considerable degree the manifestations of its philosophical foundation.

The concept of Manifest Destiny served its adherents well, so that even those who disparage it most must admit that it was a most profitable concept. When the concept of a multitribal America dies riddled with AK47 slugs and epithets, those with orderly minds will cast about for some concept to organize their new society around. They may well look to the past. Manifest Destiny covered with a glossy coat of tribal war paint may be just the idea.

It can not be dismissed that the establishment itself will impose this solution if their amoral calculus indicates it serves their purposes. Blacks should pause from time to time and remind themselves that the establishment's abandonment of the white working class was not based on moral principles, but self-serving computation. Also, despite the oh-so-fashionable disparagement of the white working class by the wine and cheese set, these "angry white males" will remain the most potent pool of military assets in North America for some time. Should the white establishment give them the go-ahead, the blacks will not survive. An establishment imposed solution may well be a "final" solution.

Apocalypse in the North

"Negro equality! Fudge! How long, in the Government of a God great enough to make and rule the universe, shall there continue knaves to vend, and fools to quip, so low a piece of demagogism as this?"—Abraham Lincoln

The heart of America, its culture and its wealth, beats in the European, English-speaking North. Here we see the pattern of black inner cities surrounded by primarily white suburban and rural areas. Blacks will seize the municipal governments and urban blacks will become increasingly poverty-stricken due to mismanagement and corruption of black one party rule, the recent financial collapse of Washington D.C. being a case in point. Riots will increase, and black mayors will not put them down so as not to alienate their power base, just as New York's Mayor Dinkins gave his tacit blessing to the Crown Heights riot of 1991. Consider this quote from an article by John Taylor in *New York Magazine* entitled *The Pogrom Papers*:[1]

> "Not only were Jews singled out for attack—a necessary but not a sufficient condition for a pogrom—but, just as happened during Kristallnacht, the anti-Semitic rampage seemed to the Jews on the streets to have official sanction. Police on patrol in Crown Heights, threatened with suspension if they moved from their designated positions, at times did nothing to stop the violence. A Hasidic Jew named Isaac Bitton told investigators he was walking home with his

---

1 John Taylor, "The Pogrom Papers", *New York Magazine*, Aug. 2, 1993, p. 24.

12-year-old son on Tuesday night, and asked police if Schenectady Ave. was safe. They assured him it was. But an aggressive crowd on the other side of the avenue approached him. He was hit with a brick and fell. The mob pulled his son away and beat him. This all took place in view of the police. 'One resident on the street saw the incident from her window and screamed for the police to help them.' The report says. 'The police, she says, did not come to their assistance.'"

When some citizens sued the city over this withholding of police protection, city attorneys responded thusly in court: "The plaintiff simply had no constitutional or federal right to have the police respond to their calls for assistance or to receive police protection against potential harm caused by private parties."[2]

This breathtaking response gives us a clear preview of what urban life will come to when the demographic and political transformation of our cities is completed. And bear in mind that you won't be allowed any firearm to defend yourself. In fact, if you dare to, the police will arrest you.

Let me repeat that quote again, so hopefully you will feel the full weight of the words:

"The plaintiff simply had no constitutional or federal right to have the police respond to their calls for assistance or to receive police protection against potential harm caused by private parties."

Crimes of all sorts will increase, driving out whites. The surrounding white areas will grow increasingly radical. Walled suburbs will spread as America takes on the appearance of medieval Europe. As in the South, white militias will form.

Our government and institutions will effectively abolish many of our traditional liberties—such as freedom of speech, and the right to bear arms—to appease radical blacks. White and black police will clash with each other, first within police departments. Later, white suburban and black city police will

---

2 *The New York Times*, June 28, 1993, p. 3.

have firefights where their boundaries meet. Predominantly white national guard units will likewise clash with black city police in the course of putting down riots.

These racial firefights will escalate in frequency, duration and scope as black police departments acquire the armaments of armies in order to control urban riots, but also to give radical black mayors an intimidating bargaining chip in negotiations with the white federal government. If anyone thinks a second civil war has not crossed the minds of black Mayors, they should ponder this quote from a 1988 interview with Detroit's mayor, Coleman Young:[3]

Interviewer (of the Canadian Broadcasting Corp.): What would happen if you went door to door and started collecting all the guns?

(Mayor Young responded that he had no objection to confiscating guns as long as it was done equally in both black and white areas. Then he continued.)

Mayor Young: "... but I'll be damned if I'm going to let them collect guns in the city of Detroit while we're surrounded by hostile suburbs and the whole rest of the state who have guns, where you have vigilantes, practicing Ku Klux Klan in the wilderness with automatic weapons."

The New York Times article that this quote appeared in had the telling title: "The battle lines are clear and dangerous: the white suburbs vs. the black city." Battle lines, automatic weapons, surrounded, whites vs. blacks.—all these sound as if they were lifted from the dispatches of two dying nations locked in war.

Eventually, open warfare will erupt. Open war may erupt when minority politicians and their radical, leftist allies seize power in federal elections, precipitating total disintegration

---

3 *The New York Times*, "The Battle Lines are Clear and Dangerous: The White Suburbs vs. the Black City", July 29, 1990, Sect. 6, p. 26.

of our regular military along racial lines. Or, it may erupt when gangs or armed cults such as the Nation of Islam declare independence for the cities they control.

On the face of it, the blacks in the cities confront an insurmountable military disadvantage. First, most heavy weapons are at this time located in federal military bases outside the cities in predominately white areas, and therefore should fall primarily into the hands of white formations. Also, cities are completely dependent on food, water, fuel and electrical power that must constantly flow in from surrounding areas inhabited by whites. As these are easy to cut off, the cities should be quickly reduced to nothing but masses of freezing, starving targets subject to artillery bombardment at the discretion of white besiegers, something like Sarajevo in Bosnia.

However, demographics and other circumstances may well tilt the balance of power to the blacks. If the federal government is captured by an alliance of radical whites and minorities, they may prudently transfer heavy weapons to military bases loyal to them. Also, the federal military will be primarily minority by the time of Civil War II in the north. A minority-dominated federal military and the military formations of southern blacks might well have more firepower than white suburban and rural populations who may well be without privately-owned firearms by the time these events come to pass. It is clear that in a straight up black versus white confrontation in the north, the blacks loose. This reality dictates a strategy of a black alliance with establishment white imperialists, and internationalists. This is a high risk strategy because blacks will almost certainly be thrown overboard by the establishment if the percentage of their population decreases, and it may well result in a white genocidal fury against them if it is unsuccessful and the whites win. If the blacks are initially successful, white guerrillas will certainly fight back. Again, these events will not occur in isolation. Canada, which itself may break up into English-speaking and French-speaking sections, may provide sanctuaries for white guerrilla formations. Foreign governments may give assistance to either side as their self-interests dictate, and the UN may occupy parts of America.

The demographic pressures and racial conflict that are propelling the northern section of America into Civil War II are all to easy to see. On the other hand, it is impossible to make confident predictions about the complex set of circumstances that will give victory to one side or the other because time and demographics are eroding the military potential of northern whites. Still, on the whole, the prospects of the white revolutionaries appear better. It is in the North that the final and climatic battle over the carcass of imperial America will be fought, and an exclusively white nation will likely arise. The black cities will either be wiped out or allowed autonomy, perhaps in confederation with the black South.

The Tribal Armies of Civil War II

"Well, I don't know if they'll frighten the enemy or not, but they certainly frighten me."—Lord Wellington after inspecting his troops.

How will the armies that fight Civil War II come into being? Who will join them, and why, and where will they get their weapons? America is saturated with armed organizations that will blossom into the tribal armies of Civil War II: The Army, the Navy, the Air Force, the Marines, the Coast Guard, their reserve components, and fifty state national guards. The Border Patrol, the Secret Service, the BATF, the DEA, the FBI, the CIA and U.S. Marshals. All totalled, there are 46 civilian agencies of the federal government that have agents who carry guns and have the power to make arrests.[1] Don't go away; there's more.

State police, county police, city police, housing police, transit police, Indian reservation police, prison guards, and private security companies. (And now for the tribal party animals!)

The Mafia, the Colombian cocaine cartels, Jamaican posses, The Ghost Shadows, the Flying Dragons, anti-Castro paramilitary units, Moslem terrorist cells, the Jewish Defense League, the Fruit of Islam, the Ku Klux Klan, neo-Nazis, the Christian Identity movement, armed religious cults, the Black Guerrilla Family, Crips, Bloods, the Gangster Disciples, the

---

1 *Harper's Magazine*, "Harper's Index", June, 1995, p. 11.

Black Disciples, the Latin Disciples, the Latin Kings, the Simon City Royals, the Mexican Mafia, the Big Time Criminals, Hispanics Causing Panic, the LA Boyz, the Netas, the Zulu Nation, the Jungle Boys, the Jungle Brothers, the Abdullahs, Los Solidos, the Hazard Gang, the Nuestra Familia, United Raza, the Fresno Bulldogs, the Two Sixers, the Insane Deuces, the Insane Unknowns, 20 Love, the Bottoms Boys, the Vice Lords, the Harpys, the Aryan Brotherhood, the Aryan Nations, the White Patriot Party, the Michigan Militia, the Blue Ridge Hunt Club, the Alabama Militia, the Arizona Militia, the Butte County Militia, the Indiana Militia, the Michigan Militia, the Montana Militia, the Georgia Militia, the Oregon Militia, the Colorado Free Militia, the Texas Constitutional Militia, the Carbineers, the Minnesota Patriots Council, the Texas Emergency Reserve, the Alabama Minutemen, the Special Forces Underground, Hell's Angels, Banditos, the Gypsy Jokers, Pagans, Warlocks, the International Posse, the Black Panther Militia, the Aryan Republican Army, White Aryan Resistance, the Islamic Liberation Army, the Freemen, skinheads, and other armed groups too numerous to mention. These fellows are not the sort of chaps one would invite to tea with Her Majesty. On the other hand, they are just the kind of all-American guys to play Civil War II from kickoff to champagne. These belligerent groups are almost all ethnically oriented, and our police departments are increasingly becoming ethnically oriented as well. Unless present trends reverse themselves, even the federal agencies and federal military will be racially oriented and polarized. Not a pretty picture. America is plainly splitting up into armed camps along ethnic fault lines, but no one seems to have noticed, certainly not the establishment media. Why? To this witch's brew one must add all the firepower. First stir in the untold number of guns and heavy weapons in the hands of the armed forces and police. Then shovel in the estimated 200 million[2] privately-held firearms, just about one for every adult in the United States of America. In California in 1993, 665,229 firearms were sold legally. That's 1,873 per day.

About two-thirds were handguns, which means that the remaining one third, or about 600 per day, were shotguns or rifles.[3] That means that every day in 1993 enough shotguns and rifles were sold in California to equip an infantry battalion. I say again:

Every day in California, enough rifles and shotguns were sold to equip an infantry battalion . . . an infantry battalion of Civil War II.

California is the odds-on favorite to kick off Civil War II, and one cannot disparage the Californians for lack of preparedness. And that's just the legal stuff. How much else is coming across the border and being sold on the black market?

---

2 Edward F. Dolan, Marc Aret, and M. Scariano, *Guns in the United States*, F. Watts Publishers, 1994, p. 8.

3 *Congressional Quarterly Research Reports*, "Gun Control" by Richard L. Worsnop, Jan. 1994 to Dec. 1994, p. 507.

Urban Street Gangs

"The instinctive need to be the member of a closely-knit group fighting for common ideals may grow so strong that it becomes inessential what these ideals are."—Konrad Lorenz

Street gangs will doubtless form the core of future black and Hispanic urban militias. Consider these particulars of urban street gangs:

1. They are self-financed by the drug trade.
2. They are ethnically oriented.
3. They are heavily armed.
4. They are organized and disciplined. They have constitutions that ensure organizational survival despite the death and imprisonment of their leaders.
5. They are numerous almost beyond belief. The Los Angeles Sheriff has files on 100,000 gang members. San Antonio has an estimated 5,000 gang members. Chicago has an estimated 50,000 gang members. Malcolm Klein, perhaps America's leading authority on street gangs, estimates that there are over 400,000 street gang members in America, all totaled.[1] Attorney General Janet Reno has put the figure in excess of 500,000 gang members nationwide in 16,000 different gangs. She has said that in 1993 they committed 580,000 gang-related crimes.[2]

---

1 *Scholastic Update*, "Girls in the Hood" by Gini Sikes, Feb. 11, 1994, p. 20.
2 *New Jersey Star Ledger*, May 14, 1996, p. 8.

6. Their leadership is composed of courageous, industrious and intelligent young men—not dim-witted punks as commonly depicted by Hollywood—because promotion is based exclusively on leadership, business acumen, and successful application of ruthless violence.

Without anyone noticing it, these urban gangs have evolved into large formations of light infantry. In their organization, discipline, aggressiveness, manpower and firepower, they are almost indistinguishable from formal armies. Let me say that again so that hopefully it hits you like somebody pounding a nail into your head with a hammer: *These urban gangs are evolving into serious armies, armies hostile to the established government.*

The only significant difference between these urban gangs and armies is that the gangs exist for criminal purposes. Should their primary objectives become political, and many are becoming involved in politics, then these gangs will be instantly transformed into real armies.

These gangs cannot be eliminated by any amount of police activity, just as police activity never succeeded in eliminating the Mafia. These gangs were conceived in, and thrive in, the environment of vast, desperately poor and densely-packed slums—slums neglected and abandoned by the establishment. These gangs have a lucrative monopoly on the drug trade in these slums, and are thus self-propelled, financially. They are steadily growing in financial power, firepower, manpower, and sophistication. They are now beginning to branch out into other illegal activities such as protection rackets, labor union corruption, and political corruption just as the Mafia did.

The Mafia thrived in the huge slums of Italian immigrants, but the Italians assimilated and moved to the suburbs, and the Mafia has eroded in proportion. The huge black and Hispanic slums are not shrinking, they are expanding, and the gangs are growing in proportion. These minority ghettos are permanent and expanding fixtures of our society, and their expansion beyond a certain indefinable extent means inevitable civil war.

When considering gangs, it is necessary to note that many of their activities are political in nature. Money from protection rackets are a form of taxation, and the protection provided from rival gangs is a form of police protection. Labor union takeovers by gangs are a form of organizing society. That these activities are illegal does not invalidate this fact.

These gangs are establishing economic, social, legal, and even military structures that parallel the legal structures that connect the ghettos to the rest of American society, and these illegal structures are displacing their legal counterparts which have ceased to function in any meaningful way, except to serve as siphon hoses sucking money out of the ghetto inhabitants and into the pockets of the politically connected.

The establishment sanctions some minority structures in a lame attempt at co-option, and to provide a sort of counterbalance to the illegal and clearly anti-establishment minority organizations such as gangs and the Nation of Islam. Typically, leaders such as the Rev. Jesse Jackson receive large grants of tax money, corporate money, foundation money, air time on the establishment media, and fawning praise from establishment politicians. That the Rev. Jackson neither vomits nor breaks out in howls of laughter during these disgusting displays of self-flagellation and sucking up is testimony to his amazing self-control.

If you're still not convinced that these urban street gangs pose a real threat to professional police and soldiers, think again. In Bosnia, Moslem criminal gangs scored the initial victories against the Yugoslav Army, taking their garrisons under siege and capturing their heavy weapons that provided the backbone of the fledgling Bosnian Army.[3]

---

3 *The New York Times*, October 4, 1993, p. 3; *The New York Times*, October 27, 1993, p. 6.

Recently in Grozny, most of the fighters came from gangs transformed into heavily-armed militias, and it took the mighty Russian Army approximately three months to drive them out of Grozny despite leveling the city with air strikes and artillery that at times reached 4,000 impacts an hour.[4] In fact, in the initial assault, entire units of the professional Russian Army were wiped out to the last man. Dogs roamed the streets eating the dead while the elderly starved and froze in damp cellars. It should also be noted that the local police sided with these gang-militias to fight the Russian invaders, just as our police will eventually side with their co-ethnics.

The Russian government was faced with the reality that they had to level Grozny or accept a humiliating defeat at the hands of militias. Their choice is history, and provides us with a preview of what will happen to our own cities should the ghetto street gangs ever aspire to political goals.

Actually, America's street gangs have already begun to take on political goals. In Chicago in 1995, two (avowedly) former members of the Gangster Disciples ran for seats on the city council.[5] One gangster-candidate was Wallace "Gator" Bradley, a convicted felon and ex-con. Both lost by 2 to 1 vote margins, but they resolved to try again. A political group tied to the Gangster Disciples bought 300 shirts, ties, skirts and blouses for the campaign workers to wear. This is an expected milestone on the march towards Civil War II, so watch for more direct political action by street gangs.

On April 5, 1994, some 200 leading members of New York's black and Hispanic street gangs met in a theater in Harlem with two members of New York's black political establishment, the Rev. Al Sharpton and Eric Adams, the head of the Guardians, an association of black New York City police officers.[6]

---

4 *New York Review of Books*, "Killing Chechnya" by Frederick C. Cuny, April 6, 1995, p. 14.
5 *The New York Times*, April 6, 1995, p. 20.

Officially, they were there to discuss ways to end violence in the streets. This avowed reason was nothing but fluff for the media. In reality, they were there to promote their mutual interests. Military power, which the gangs possess, is the foundation of political power, which the Rev. Sharpton and Officer Adams have and want more of. Political power, which Sharpton and Adams have, will lend legitimacy to the gangs.

But this alliance of gangsters and politicians goes beyond this immediate goal of mutual reinforcement. Viewed from the proper perspective, this conjunction of gangsters and politicians comes into sharper focus. To create a nation, several fundamental items are required.

First, you must have a large body of people who mutually recognize each other as co-nationals. Second, they must reside together in a land where they are the majority. Third, you must have a political establishment of some sort. Fourth, you must have a military force to defend your land. The gangsters and the politicians brought together the final two elements necessary for the creation of an embryonic nation— the military power of the gangs and the political organization of Sharpton and Adams.

Another such convention occurred on May 1, 1993 in Los Angeles featuring the Crips and the Bloods. A week later, the Rev. Benjamin Chavis, then executive director of the NAACP, attended a similar national gang summit in Kansas City, Missouri.[7] In October 1993, Jesse Jackson attended a "National Truce Summit" of street gangs in Chicago,[8] and told the gangsters that they represented the "new frontier of the civil rights struggle." The plain truth is that we are seeing the first examples of establishment black leaders bidding for the military backing of the gangs. We will see much more of this unholy courtship in the future.

---

6 *The New York Post*, April 6, 1994, p. 16.
7 *The New York Times*, May 2, 1993, Sect. I, p. 1.
8 *The New Jersey Star Ledger*, October 25, 1993, Sect. P, p. 14.

Watch for the first public protest demonstration by gang members, which will further signal that the gangs are taking on political goals. If any black politicians attend it will be a clear sign that the street gangs and black politicians do indeed have a common agenda, a common political and military agenda. Also, watch for the first reports of gangs organizing themselves along military lines, drawing up plans for defense of their areas against the police and military, wearing military uniforms, assuming military ranks, standardizing their weapons, and any other indications that they are beginning to re-invent themselves as political and/or military organizations.

These gangs have even infiltrated the very organizations that are supposedly going to protect us from them during Civil War II. According to the *Chicago Sun Times*, in the last three years 15 Chicago policemen have been charged with crimes, forced to resign or investigated for membership in a street gang. Here's how Chicago Police Superintendent Matt Rodriguez summed up the situation:

> "We can't deny we have individuals who are members, fraternize or associate with street gangs. Why would they not do the same things organized crime always did, such as infiltrate the police? If the mob bought judges, politicians and policemen, why do we think the gangs can't do it?"[9]

Incredibly, the Chicago police brass now allows known and even self-admitted gang members to masquerade as police because the police brass claim they can not fire these gangster/cops until they actually violate a law. Why can't they fire them for lying on their applications? Presumably, applicants are asked if they belonged to street gangs. Why can't the police brass use the RICO anti-conspiracy laws to get rid of these gangster/cops?

---

9 *The Los Angeles Times*, Oct. 8, 1995, p. 16. This references and quotes the *Chicago Times* article.

Regrettably, we must seriously ask if some gangs are now more disciplined, better organized and less corrupt than some of our urban police departments. If we compare what is probably our premier gang, the Gangster Disciples, to what is probably our worst major police department, the New Orleans police, it's clear that the Gangster Disciples are by far the superior organization. Even as our gangs are growing in size, becoming more sophisticated, and better organized and armed, our police departments are headed in the opposite direction, steadily growing more corrupt, less organized, and less disciplined. To any sober and objective observer, it's clear where these two ongoing trends are taking us. From a purely military perspective, the urban gangs could probably defeat some of our urban police departments right now, today, if they acted in concert. If you think not, recall that there are an estimated 100,000 gangs members in Los Angeles. I have no idea of how many police there are in Los Angeles, but it must be less because there are only 554,000 police on all state and local police forces in all of America,[10] and Attorney General Janet Reno estimates that there are 500,000 street gang members nationwide. The smart money would have to be on the gangs, at least until the National Guard and probably the federal military as well came galloping to the rescue of the outnumbered and out-gunned police.

If you want an ongoing example of a street gang undergoing a classic transformation into a political/military organization, just consider the Chicago-based Gangster Disciples, and their leader, Larry Hoover.[11] Hoover, 45, has been in the belly of the Illinois prison system for 22 years for murder, but that has not stopped him from running the 50,000 member Gangster Disciples who are spread over 35 states and who

10 *The Atlantic Monthly*, "The Crisis of Public Order", by Adam Walinsky, July, 1995, p. 39.
11 *Newsweek*, "The 'Disciples' of Drugs—And Death" by John McCormick, Feb. 5, 1996, p. 56.

take in possibly as much as $500 million a year, primarily through drug sales. They have a 42 page Constitution and a seven-tiered organizational structure with Chairman Hoover at the zenith and two separate Boards of Directors. They've put candidates on Chicago ballots and organized a protest march on City Hall. Hoover now "lives and breathes politics," reads Machiavelli, and studies how the late Chicago mayor Richard Daley put together his political machine.

During the Al Capone era, the mob murder rate for Chicago topped out at 75 in 1926. Police now estimate that the Gangster Disciples kill that many every year. This means that Larry Hoover has probably ordered the execution, directly or indirectly, of well over 1,000 people. The federal and all the state governments combined have not executed that many people during the last twenty years. Of all American institutions, probably only the federal military has killed more people than Larry Hoover during the last two decades, and those were almost all foreigners. Mr. Larry Hoover is certainly America's most "productive" living murderer, and arguably the greatest murderer in all American history, but I've only seen his name in print once. Think about that! Arguably the greatest murderer in American history is right now in absolute control of a near-army of 50,000 armed men, yet he has less name recognition than President Clinton's cat. Mark my words, the establishment media will not change their perception of these organizations from that of street gangs to ethnic militias until a gang like the Gangster Disciples defeats one of our major city's police departments, takes over Los Angeles or Chicago, and tears down the American flag. By that time it will be too late.

The federal military itself has been infiltrated by street gangs. According to *Newsweek* magazine[12] these gangs are active in the Army, Navy, Air Force, and Marines. They are

---

12 *Newsweek*, "Gangstas in the Ranks", July 24, 1995, p. 48.

active at more than 50 American military bases. They stake out "turf" on aircraft carriers, and gang members were photographed flashing gang hand signs during the Persian Gulf War. On Dec. 4, 1992, gang members, including an army specialist 4th class, hacked a man and his three small children to death, one an infant, to protect a gang drug operation.

The Army and Air Force have issued a training manual to aid their investigators in combating stepped-up infiltration by gangs. The manual includes photographs and descriptions of gang hand recognition signals, a glossary of gang slang, and information about gang colors. This is the military that is supposed to hold the country together in Civil War II, a military that can scarcely hold itself together today.

Gangs have even started to appear on Indian reservations. The Pima reservation at Salt River, Arizona had 55 drive by shootings in 1994.[13] Some of these Indian gangs are branches of black and Hispanic urban gangs.

Mao Tse-tung approved of recruiting bandits into his revolutionary army, and he also noted that unsuccessful guerrillas armies had a tendency to devolve into bandit gangs. Pancho Villa started out as a bandit. Even the admirers of our own Civil War I guerrillas are hard pressed to defend them against charges of banditry.[14] As with nations and empires, there is a spectrum that starts with plain banditry on one end and runs to pure revolutionary military formations at the other. Bandit gangs evolve into armies, and armies devolve into bandit gangs.

One such Serb bandit/soldier is Zeljko Raznatovic, better known by his favorite alias from his criminal days, "Arkan." Even those who disparage Arkan most have to admit that he is a most productive gangster who racked up an impressive

---

13 *The New York Times*, March 18, 1995, p. 1.
14 The story of one such famous guerrilla is unabashedly related in *Under the Black Flag*, by Captain Kit Dalton, available from Larry Tolbert, PO Box 241654, Memphis, TN 38124

string of bank robberies, contract murders, and jailbreaks blazing with gunfire all over Europe. Back in Yugoslavia, he murdered a policeman, but so dazzled the communists powers-that-be that they put him on the payroll as an assassin. When the war in Yugoslavia broke out, Arkan quickly set up a militia, using a small Mafia he had built up as the core. Arkan and his Tiger militia butchered entire villages of Croats and Moslems, raping young girls in front of their parents, then machine-gunning the lot. His army of psychopaths is self-financed by looting, and has grown like a cancer.

In Sarajevo, Bosnia, two criminal gangs grew so rich from smuggling, black marketeering, drugs and prostitution, that they quickly evolved into full-blown armies. In fact, the government made their leaders into army officers and their gangs into the 9th and 10th Mountain Brigades, and assigned them the responsibility of the city's front line defenses on the critical Trebevic mountain. Eventually, it came to the point that these two gangs were so powerful that the legitimate Bosnian government had to move against them or count the days until the gangsters moved on them. The two gang leaders, Musan Topalovic and Ramiz Delalic, were forced to surrender after fighting between their backers and government forces that left downtown Sarajevo a combat zone.

Our American gangs lack only one item that prevents them from being a match for our federal military in street fighting. They still lack armaments such as antitank and antiaircraft weapons that allowed the street gangs and militias of Grozny to bloody the nose of the professional Russian army.

This deficiency has not entirely escaped their attention. In 1986, the El Rukns, a black Chicago street gang, attempted to buy plastic explosives and a bazooka from an underground arms dealer.[15] The arms dealer was actually an FBI agent, and

---

15 The New York Times, Oct. 31, 1986, p. 12; Nov. 5, 1987, p. 16; Nov. 25, 1987, p. 16.

several of the El Rukns were sentenced to prison when a raid on an El Runk headquarters uncovered three automatic weapons and a store of hand grenades. The El Rukns intended to commit terrorist acts on American soil paid for by the Libyan government.

The U.S. Justice Department held a "Street Gang Symposium" in Johnstown, Pennsylvania in November 1994. According to *Newsweek* magazine[16] this gathering produced a report warning that:

"Some gangs have access to highly sophisticated personal weapons such as grenades, machine guns, rocket launchers and military explosives."

When civil authority breaks down in America, our criminal gangs will instantly fill the power vacuum, just exactly as has been the pattern in other lands. The gangs have the organization and firepower to serve as the nucleus for actual armies. And since they will be self-financed in the coming time of chaos, they will grow like wildfire. Militias, cults like the Nation of Islam, and other armed organizations will also rapidly grow into full-blown armies.

If establishment leaders are not able to quickly reestablish central control prior to the evolution of gangs into armies, the government may be defeated in initial encounters, and America may undergo a prolonged period of tribal and gang-driven anarchy before any sort of national order is reestablished, either by the gang/armies or the establishment. Watch for more attempts by street gangs to acquire heavy weapons and their conjunctions with foreign governments, foreign terrorist organizations and—worst of all—American politicians.

16 *Newsweek*, July 24, 1995.

Our Military Bases Fall to Siege

"It (the Siegfried Line) is a monument to human stupidity. When natural obstacles—oceans and mountains—can be so readily overcome, anything that man makes, man can overcome."—Gen. George S. Patton Jr. 1944

Those skeptical about the ability of mobs and guerrillas to overthrow our government will point out its professional police and military, its great stores of heavy weapons, and its numerous military bases, and conclude that lightly-armed guerrillas and amateur militias have no chance of success. This line of reasoning, while reassuring, is mere bean counting. Practical and historic examination of the perceived military strengths of the federal government reveals them as fatal weakness that will only hasten its downfall. Our military bases are a case in point. Since they're sited on supposedly friendly American soil, they weren't designed to withstand sieges. To withstand a siege, certain fundamental features are required:

First: A cleared field of fire outside the outermost defensive perimeter to deny cover and concealment to besieging forces. Our military bases often abut cities or suburbs that extend right up to the outer perimeter. Others are surrounded by hilly and wooded terrain that will likewise provide ample cover for future besiegers.

Second: They must have a serious defensive perimeter consisting of such features as mine fields and bunkers for heavy weapons. Our military bases typically have a chain link fence and nothing more.

Third: They must have sufficient manpower, preferably dedicated infantry, to man the defensive perimeter. Our bases are typically guarded by a handful of security guards.

Fourth: They should have hardened, on-base facilities for storage of food, water, and ammunition sufficient to last out sieges. They should have securely-located internal runways and hellipads for resupply by air during a siege. Critical command and control buildings should be hardened and located at some distance from the outermost perimeter.

Few, if any, of our in-country bases have all of these features; many have none. Typically, they're dependent on outside sources for food, water, and electricity which will be easily cut off by besiegers. Typically, their security is designed to stop nothing more than the occasional burglar. Vietnam veterans will testify to the contrast between our fire bases in Vietnam that bristled with weapons and our poorly-defended in-country military bases. In fact many will be tempting targets for guerrillas seeking an easy source of heavy weapons and helpless federal troops to slaughter. It is instructive to recall that in Civil War I, all but three federal military bases in the south were quickly captured by state national guards or cobbled together militias, and the heavy weapons taken provided the backbone of the new Confederate Army.

The same pattern recently repeated itself in Yugoslavia. I was stationed at one federal military base that had been captured by rebel forces with little difficulty. The base was a small supply depot, about half a block wide and three blocks long. It was sited on the edge of a small village. Its only security was a chain link fence and an amusing little mine field about four feet wide.

The base had been manned by about 80 soldiers, mostly reluctant conscripts, and many were co-ethnics of the villagers who were secretly planning to take the base. A federal soldier, an NCO, secretly sided with the villagers and dispatched many of the base's soldiers to an off-base gymnasium to play soccer on the day of the attack, an order the bored conscripts happily obeyed. About twenty villagers armed with homemade shotguns, some stolen AK47s and a few scoped sniper rifles occupied a hill overlooking the base and opened fire.

The soldiers replied with machine guns and rocket propelled grenades, but without much effect on the attackers who were dispersed and well concealed behind trees. The base commander, cut off from outside help, without stores of food or water, surrendered to a force inferior in numbers and firepower, but superior in all other respects.

If the episode sounds humorous, be advised that such incidents are not untypical of real civil wars, regardless of how Hollywood Rambos fight wars on television'. It illustrates that in a civil war the hearts and minds of the combatants count for a lot. And how did these villagers get the military knowledge necessary to capture a military base manned by professionals? Why from the Yugoslav army of course. Most were army veterans, and they were led by an ex-Yugoslav Army officer. This pattern will be repeated many times in our next civil war.

In our Civil War II, federal military bases will likewise be taken under siege by ethnic militias, and many of the federal defenders will be co-ethnics of the attackers. There will be numerous instances of defenders siding with the attackers, supplying them with information, deserting with their weapons, and even turning their assault rifles on their own comrades and officers. Vietnam veterans will again be familiar with this difficulty that led to the fall of many a South Vietnamese firebase.

Our Police and Military Divide and Clash

"Why does Col. Grigsby refer to me to learn how to deal with mutineers? He should have them shot where they stand." —Stonewall Jackson's response when asked how to proceed with soldiers who refused orders.

Neither are the police of much long range comfort to the government. In fact, some police departments will be among the first organized groups to attack the federal government. Watch to see if our police voluntarily divide into ethnically-based groups hostile to each other. If they do, Civil War II is that much closer.

Actually, many of our urban police have already divided themselves into ethnically exclusive and mutually hostile organizations called associations, one for each ethnic group. And the minority associations are successfully blocking the recruitment and advancement of white officers by racist affirmative action. Minority politicians are seizing control of the major cities, and accelerating this purging of whites from their police departments.

Urban police departments will become almost exclusively minority. The police outside the cities will remain primarily white. Armed clashes between police of different ethnic groups will occur, first between policemen within the same police department, and later between separate and ethnically exclusive police departments where their jurisdictions meet.

Should our regular federal military likewise divide along ethnic lines, we will be past the point of no return towards Civil War II. Actually, it appears that racial associations have begun to appear in our military. On April 30, 1995, the television program *Sixty Minutes* reported that an underground magazine called *The Resister* was quietly circulating in Ft. Bragg, North Carolina and other American Army bases.

The Resister is put out by the Special Forces Underground,[1] a clandestine group of the United States Army's elite Green Berets. The Green Berets interviewed by *Sixty Minutes* believe that the constitutional rights of Americans are being illegally violated by the federal government. In *The Resister*, these Green Berets are discussing the possibility and means of resisting the federal establishment by armed force, including guerrilla warfare. The appearance of the Special Forces Underground is ominously significant because the Green Berets are the military's primary counterinsurgency force, the very ones who will be assigned to track down and eliminate anti-government guerrillas in Civil War II.

It is predictable that the military brass will use the appearance of *The Resister* as an excuse to politicize the Green Berets, and that they will instruct affirmative action officers who are mostly minority to purge the Green Berets of conservative white soldiers and replace them with radicals and minorities carefully screened for political reliability, exactly as in the old Soviet Union.

Any who doubt that our military is being racialized and politicized should read an article by a Mr. C. J. Chivers that appeared in the Oct. 16, 1995 issue of *The Nation* magazine. In this article titled "Looking For A Few Good (Black) Men,"[2]

---

1   Featured on the television program *Sixty Minutes*, April 30, 1995. A subscription to *The Resister*, the newsletter of the Special Forces Underground is $25 per year. Send a check or money order with the payee line blank to: PO Box 47095, Kansas City, MO 64188.

2   *The Nation*, "Looking For A Few Good (Black) Men", Oct. 16, 1995,

Mr. Chivers enthusiastically described his activities while a Marine Corps captain assigned to recruiting officer candidates:

> "I was actively discriminating against whites. While selecting college students for officer candidate school, I routinely turned down long lines of qualified white males to save room for blacks. I denied whites interviews. Every few months I threw stacks of their resumes into the trash."

Recall that empires often employ elite military units for internal counterinsurgency. The Green Berets are being politicized, and we are perhaps witnessing the birth of America's elite internal counterinsurgency force, something like Russia's elite internal counterinsurgency force, the infamous MVD Internal Security that perpetrated the rape of Grozny. In fact, our entire military is being racialized and the message will not be lost on other white military personnel who will form other clandestine organizations in reaction, which will be used as a pretext for yet more purging and politicizing of our military.

In fact, this politicizing is going on right now in the form of "discrimination hotlines" used to turn in whites accused of racism. "Sensitivity" classes are used to intimidate whites and ferret out and discharge those whites who can not be intimidated. Watch for more allegations of racism to purge conservative white officers and men, more "sensitivity" (brainwashing) classes, racist affirmative action programs, and racial quotas to racialize and politicize our federal military.

Our current system of racist recruiting and promotion means that every minority officer, NCO and soldier knows that he owes his rank not to his own merit, but to an artificially maintained system of racist special privileges. Should any political reform movement gain power in Washington and

p. 428.

attempt to dismantle this racist system, minority officers and soldiers will be tempted to attempt a *coup d'etat* or face losing their special privileges. If the minority soldiers and radical white soldiers outnumber the non-radical whites, America will become a military dictatorship and race war will erupt.

Gen. Colin Powell rose to the ultimate military position of Chairman of the Joint Chiefs of Staff not entirely on merit, but partly because he was black, but few dare say this out loud. When Louis Farrakhan asked Gen. Powell to join his Million Man march on Washington D.C., Gen. Powell declined and cited "schedule conflicts." This is exactly the same as some prominent German declining to march with a pre-1933 Hitler, not because he objected to Hitler's psychotic racism (which parallels Farrakhan's), but merely because he was busy elsewhere.

It is also no surprise that someone with Gen. Powell's demonstrated lack of character favors racist affirmative action. As revealed by the Oct. 6, 1995 issue of the *New York Daily News*, in 1985 Gen. Powell was one of a group of prominent blacks who bought WKBW-TV, a Buffalo, New York television station, taking advantage of special tax breaks not available to whites. Blacks are making much progress in their racist agenda to gain exemption from taxation (as illustrated by Gen. Powell's above manipulation) while simultaneously siphoning off more government aid intentionally channelled to blacks but not to whites.[3]

It should also be noted that Gen. Powell was engaging in this "business" while on active duty and drawing government pay. Active duty military officers should not engage in private business ventures as they are a time-consuming distraction which conflicts with a professional officer's sacred duty to devote all his time and energy to looking after the defense of his country and the lives of the men entrusted to his command.

---

3 *The New York Daily News*, October 6, 1995, p. 19.

Our military is looking more and more like a third-world military force every year—corrupt, politicized, tribalized, more interested in finance than fighting, and more oriented towards putting down internal rebellions than combating foreign enemies. Our Army is currently about 40% minority, which means that it is more minority-dominated than society in general. This is not an accident. It is intended to put the ultimate power—military power—into hands beholden to the New Order. The saturating of our military with unqualified minorities and "racially sensitive" whites is being consciously and deliberately promoted by the New Order to insure that there is absolutely no chance that a reform movement can reverse the ongoing imperial conversion. When the federal military exceeds 50% minority, there will be only the smallest chance of stopping our conversion into a completely racist, undemocratic imperial dictatorship without fighting Civil War II.

The Militias

"A revolution is not a bed of roses. A revolution is a struggle to the death between the future and the past."—Fidel Castro

Militia members should make an objective analysis of current and future military and political realities. Without an accurate view of the overall picture, they will make costly errors in their organizational structure, public relations, focus of efforts, and all other areas of endeavor.

The primary reality which their every act must take into account is the increasing repression and violence of the government. Imperial conversion will accelerate month by month, possibly to the point where an entirely imperial system is in place, and key militia leaders are assassinated upon detection.

While implosion into ethnic warfare prior to that point is by far the more likely scenario, completed conversion into a fully imperial system prior to the outbreak of all-out warfare is a significant possibility. Technically considered, completed imperial conversion must be assumed because its real possibility constitutes a worst case scenario that places a limiting parameter on every facet of militia activity. Directly put, militia members must realize that there may come a day when federal agents assassinate them upon detection, or even suspicion.

Some will point out the Weaver case and claim that we've already reached that stage. This is not the case. If it were, the streets would be littered with the bodies of militiamen and other perceived enemies of the establishment. While federal conduct in the Weaver affair was nothing less than criminal terrorism, this incident should not be used as a vehicle for anti-government propaganda to the point that it clouds analysis. The firefight at Ruby Ridge should rather be viewed as a preview of what will come to be an everyday reality as conditions deteriorate.

These are difficult times for America, and things will grow worse. Therefore, all concerned should discipline themselves to the point of cold objectivity so that no false pictures are formed. Militiamen, be advised that your lives, liberty, and property are at risk, and clear thinking is a military asset as surely as guns or ammunition. While the federal government is increasingly abandoning observance of the law when circumstances permit, powerful forces still impede its plans. Americans still have trial by jury, some of our press has not been entirely co-opted by the establishment, most local police have not been militarized, many politicians are still relatively independent, and many citizens still have firearms. However, the imperialist tide is clearly eroding these foundations of liberty, and the current is increasing. Incidents like Waco and Ruby Ridge should be viewed in the light of technical analysis.

We are now in a pre-revolutionary stage of intermittent government intimidation and even criminal terrorism when the establishment calculates the circumstances are right. Because circumstances will increasingly favor establishment control of every facet of our society, militiamen should anticipate this trend and adopt organizational structures that ensure their future survival under these conditions. That's the concept, and those who fail to put it at the center of their outlook are putting themselves at unnecessary risk.

All existing militias should disband immediately, without exception. Wearing uniforms, assembling with firearms, marching, assuming military ranks, and all other militia-like activities should be discontinued. However, they should keep their weapons and encourage fellow patriots to retain theirs and acquire even more weapons. I respect the right of the people to have firearms and to form themselves into militias.

I admire the patriotism of the majority of the individuals who have joined militias. Still, I think the militias should disband.

Why should the militias disband in the face of ongoing imperial conversion? One great concern is that Hispanic militias may begin to form in the southwest in reaction, although there have been no reports of such militias yet. Regardless of how militias perceive themselves as constitutionalists—and I believe most are exactly that—the Hispanics and blacks are bound to perceive them by their appearance, which is overwhelmingly white, and thereby harboring hostile intentions towards them.

Also, liberty would be better served by Committees of Correspondence modeled after those that formed prior to the outbreak of our War of Independence. These committees should be defensive in philosophy and organization, not oriented as militias. These committees should consider military matters only to the point that they develop self-defense contingency plans for countering all possible terrorist and military aggression that their local community will be vulnerable to at the outbreak of hostilities, something in the nature of civil defense plans.

Individual committee members or teams should be assigned the task of gathering information about specific aspects of local self-defense and drawing up preliminary self-defense contingency plans based on that information. At regular intervals, these plans should be presented, discussed, and modified as needed. Priority should be given to developing plans for securing local infrastructure against lawless aggressor forces. Individual members or subcommittees should be assigned the task of monitoring local, national, and international events, and assessing their impact on local self-defense requirements. However, all lawless activity should be prohibited, and members breaking laws should be immediately expelled.

These committees should maintain contact with one another to coordinate their activities and to ensure political clout that may spare them harassment, physical assault, and even assassination by federal agents. One of their objectives should be a periodic national convention where they draw up a set of constitutional amendments aimed at taking all power out of the hands of the Supreme Court, NAFTA, the UN, and all other unelected bodies. Reform amendments of all sorts should be put forward. Also, a post-Civil War II Constitution should be drawn up because the reform amendments will almost certainly be squashed by the powers that be. This postwar Constitution should be drawn up now to prevent a dictatorship from rising out of the ashes of Civil War II.

The Vicious Nature of Civil War II

"The great questions of the day will be decided not by speeches and majority votes ... but by iron and blood."—Otto von Bismark.

What will Civil War II actually be like? Consider these patterns that wars usually follow: First, the more dissimilar the combatants are in race, nationality, religion, language and culture the more vicious the fighting usually is. America's wars of aggression against the Indians involved two sides that were completely dissimilar, and the results were hideous tortures and genocide. On the other hand, our first civil war, while extremely violent, was one of the least vicious wars ever fought due to the lack of these stated differences.

Civil War II will clearly be more like the Indian wars than our first civil war because wars fought by dissimilar armies inevitably produce excesses. In Civil War I, torture of prisoners and mutilation of the dead were rare. In the Indian wars and again in Vietnam, another war with dissimilar armies, such practices were employed by the fighters of both sides, sometimes even as a form of recreation.

Civil War II will degenerate into premeditated and systematic mass slaughter because other factors will also fuel its frenzy. Unlike Civil War I, but like the wars against the Indians, one of the goals will be to drive others from the lands wherein they reside, which guarantees fanatical resistance and necessitates measures sufficient to the objective.

This presence of civilians in battle zones will certainly increase the fury of Civil War II. Many will be killed accidentally, others on purpose, leading to reprisals, which will in turn lead to counter reprisals. In Civil War I, some of the most vicious fighting occurred in the border states with mixed populations where irregular bands like Quantrill's Raiders sprang up.

In Civil War I, almost all the combatants were members of the regular military. In Civil War II, many civilians, including women and children, will fight as guerrillas which will lead to their mass elimination on the grounds that they're combatants, or at least military assets, exactly as happened in My Lai, Vietnam. In Civil War II, as in Yugoslavia, many combatants will join specifically to avenge the murder of their families. I leave to your imagination the fate of captives in the hands of such warriors.

I was once asked if any of the Geneva Conventions were applied to prisoners my paratrooper unit took in Vietnam. I answered that rule 556 was generally applied. 556, I pointed out, is the caliber of the M16 assault rifle. The application was generally to the head. Such was war in the rock 'n' roll slaughterhouse, and so it shall be when Civil War II sweeps imperial America.

Men who have served in regular military organizations have a misconception that nonprofessionals are inherently inferior to regular military formations. This misconception is shared by the general public and the media who constantly use such adjectives as ragtag and disorganized when referring to guerrillas. Parade ground spit and polish are not to be confused with battlefield competence. Guerrillas, militias, and even mobs can, and often do, defeat regular armies when the circumstances are right, as was often the case in our own revolution against the British Empire.

Regular military organizations are oriented towards fighting other regular military organizations in stand-up battles, not guerrillas (or regular armies using guerrilla tactics) as testified to by our victory in Desert Storm, and our defeat by the Vietnamese. Our military has numerous large formations equipped with heavy weapons, but very few smaller Special

Forces-type units, which are pound for pound far superior at engaging guerrillas.

This inappropriate orientation of our military will continue just as it did all during Vietnam even when it was abundantly clear that it was a formula for certain disaster. There are reasons for this. Our military is a willing captive of our defense industry. As Country Joe and the Fish pointed out at Woodstock: "There's plenty of money to be made, supplying the Army with the tools of the trade."

And that money is clearly in capital intensive, big-ticket items like stealth bombers, aircraft carriers, nuclear submarines, Patriot missiles, and Star Wars gadgets, all of which have little or no utility in counterinsurgency.

To be fair, these items are required to counter ongoing foreign threats like Iraq and Russia, but there are deeper reasons that will continue to direct our military resources to these big ticket items all out of proportion to their actual need. First, many of our top military brass are simply corrupt. They go straight from retirement to the payoff of consulting for defense contractors in a form of institutionalized bribery.

Second, without huge formations to order about, there is little for our abundance of over-weight, over-age generals to do. General Schwarzkopf and his staff were just the sort of techno-managers needed in Desert Storm, but such individuals are usually worse than useless in the dispersed, small unit actions that characterize guerrilla warfare, where active and independent fighting leaders, not managers, are required.

It is clear that the federal military will embark on Civil War II with inappropriate organization and weapons. When the only tool you have is a sledge hammer, all about begins to look in dire need of smashing. The rebel guerrillas and militias, on the other hand, will certainly have a more flexible and decentralized structure bordering on chaos. The Afghan resistance groups, for instance, never united against the Russians, but fought them to a standstill nevertheless.

Guerrilla leaders will actually lead their troops, and those not killed will, unlike regular officers, be able to employ lessons learned in future actions. Rebel officers will achieve their positions based on success in actual battle, not on their ability to stay awake during staff meetings or meet the latest racial quota.

Rebel soldiers will be volunteers who will not suffer their lives being thrown away in pointless operations like American regulars in Vietnam were, thus, on the whole, increasing the efficiency of rebel operations. Federal soldiers, on the other hand, will increasingly be politicized officers and conscripts who will have ample opportunities to desert or otherwise shirk their duty.

The federal military will be ensnared in several dilemmas: If they use volunteers, they won't have sufficient manpower. If they use draftees, they'll wind up with hordes of disgruntled shirkers, just as in Vietnam.

If they resort to heavy weapons of mass destruction, they'll kill civilians and swell rebel ranks with dedicated fanatics just as they did in Vietnam. If they don't employ their heavy weapons, they'll be giving up one of their few military advantages and thereby increase federal casualties, lowering federal morale. If the federal forces consolidate their formations in large easily-defended firebases, they'll forfeit vast areas to the control of the rebels, just as we Americans did in Vietnam. If the federal government disperses its forces, they will be vulnerable to concentrated rebel attacks.

If the federal government keeps its units integrated, they'll have firefights within their own ranks. If they use segregated units, they'll be admitting that the cause they're fighting for is a fraud.

The Dynamics of Counterinsurgency

The classic political means of ending any guerrilla uprising is a co-option of the rebel base of support—instituting reforms that extend legal rights and economic opportunities to the rebellious people, at least to the extent that they cease supporting the guerrillas, who are then defeated in detail, hunted down one band after another.

When co-option is not offered or is rejected, usually only the classic military tool of genocide of the rebellious people remains, or at least the number of them sufficient that the survivors are terrorized into submission.

In our war for Independence, the arrogant establishment of the British Empire refused to co-opt the American colonists, but lacked the resolve to embark upon a campaign of genocide. They committed the classic error of thinking that professional soldiers would easily defeat so-called ragtag militias and lightly-armed guerrillas. The limeys wound up playing tag in the boondocks, much as we Americans did in Vietnam.

We Americans made no such error in dealing with the Indians, who could not have been co-opted in any case due to vast cultural differences. The Indians were never directly defeated militarily. They were ethnically cleansed until they absolutely ceased all military activity.

In Civil War I, the Confederates accepted their conventional military defeat only because they were aware that their co-option and correct treatment were assured. Had that not been the case, they would have fought on as guerrillas.

It is a stark fact that most ethnically-based revolutions can be crushed only by ethnic cleansing or similar butchery, and that's exactly how most such rebellions are in fact crushed. It is also a historic fact that the more different the two sides perceive each other, the more often the tool of genocide is employed. As for co-option, Civil War II will begin precisely because co-option is being scornfully rejected as "cultural genocide," and it will proceed directly to ethnic cleansing for the same reason.

Looting

"People who are vigorous and brutal often find war enjoyable, provided that it is a victorious war and that there is not too much interference with rape and plunder."—Bertrand Russell

Another factor will make Civil War II self-propelled, at least in its early stages, and that is looting. This was the pattern in Yugoslavia where Serb militias systematically pillaged entire villages, and then burnt down the houses so the victims would have nothing to return to. Stolen items like television sets were loaded into stolen cars and driven away. A year's salary could be gotten in a few minutes with an AK47, not to mention that old military pastime of rape.

Gangs and militias will control lucrative black markets and protection rackets, giving them much incentive to reject peace. If Civil War II breaks out during a severe economic downturn, which is almost certain, many unemployed men will find it a dramatic improvement in their lives.

America is awash in unemployed young men who are economically useless due to their lack of capital and marketable skills. While utterly useless in the economic sense, they are definitely assets in the military equation, because vigorous, motivated, and aggressive young males are exactly what are needed in infantry combat. This studied neglect of economically useless young males will continue because the economic establishment considers any investment in them a drain on their precious corporate profits, and they import H-1B non-immigrant foreigners rather than invest in young Americans. Ironic as it may seem, the establishment is actively assembling the very army that will cut their throats. But it won't be merely for worldly gain or revenge that these young men will fight to their deaths in Civil War II. It will be for something noble, for something basic to higher human nature, no matter how perversely manifested. They will be self-motivated by a sense of purpose, a sense of purpose that is now entirely absent from their dismal and aimless lives.

These young males of all races have grievances, real grievances, and lots of them. They also have guns, real guns, and lots of them. As the ancient Chinese curse goes, "May you live in interesting times!" Well, I fully expect that the sole virtue of the multiethnic American Empire will be a decided absence of boredom.

Economic Collapse

Since undemocratic and multiethnic empires are always unstable, they often topple into internal or external war when they encounter some additional source of instability. Certainly in the case of Mexico and probably America as well, that shock will be economic. If, or rather when, America undergoes a severe economic slump on the scale of the Great Depression of the 1930s, the establishment may make the mistake of cutting off various welfare and unemployment benefits in order to sustain its own luxurious life-style. This tragic miscalculation could well provoke rioting in every major city that will be impossible to stop prior to its exploding into all-out race war all across America. How many will die in Civil War II? In 1860 the population of the United States was just over 31 million. The combined battle deaths of the Union and Confederate Armies in Civil War I were approximately 215,000.[1] The U.S. Census Bureau projected population for 2050 is 393,000,000. Projecting from these figures gives us 2,678,000 battle dead for Civil War II. This figure should be regarded as a baseline minimum because Civil War I's casualties were largely reserved for military personnel. Unhappily, such will not be the case with our next civil war.

Civil War II in America will set off a super depression that will plunge the entire globe into economic chaos, which will further deepen the economic collapse here in America. The final result could well be mass starvation.

During previous wars in North America, food production was low tech and localized. Most food was produced in the vicinity it was consumed in, and every area had many people who knew how to grow food. Food production, processing, and distribution were not much dependent on outside areas. Even so, large areas of the South came close to mass starvation during our first civil war.

---

1 *The World Almanac and Book of Facts*, 1990, p. 792.

Today, our food producing system in North America is high tech, specialized, and dispersed. Electrical power for our farms is usually generated many miles away. Fuel and spare parts for the farm machinery are likewise produced at great distances from our farms, often overseas.

All the necessary items that must flow into our farms are generally produced at great distances from them. They all converge on our farms, which are themselves scattered all over America. The food produced again flows outwards in all directions to processing centers, and the processed food once again flows outwards in all directions over great distances to reach the consumers. All these steps are high tech and dispersed, a national and global web of highly specialized sub units as completely dependent upon each other as they are dispersed. Today, it is just about as impossible for communities to produce their own food with locally obtained inputs as it would be for them to produce their own space shuttle from locally fabricated components.

The disruptions of Civil War II will hamper the inflow of fertilizer, seed, spare parts, fuel and electricity into our farms. Food production will plummet, and the distribution of the little food produced will likewise be difficult, often impossible. Certainly, food will be used as a weapon and withheld from certain areas such as cities under siege.

Depending on the scope and duration of Civil War II, tens of millions could perish in a mass starvation unprecedented since the beginning of time. Millions more will die of disease due to immune systems weakened by lack of food. The very old and children will die off first. Soldiers, the most valuable and most heavily-armed portion of the population, will suffer the least.

In the worst case scenario, organized government will vanish entirely, and the fighting will degenerate into what the Germans term Bandenkreig. Bandenkreig means a war of bands, which is not to be confused with organized guerrilla warfare. In Bandenkreig, independent, roving bands battle each other for access to food, loot, liquor, rape, and sheer survival, something akin to futuristic Australian films such as *Mad Max*.

Bandenkreig is no mere downunder hallucination. Bandenkreig is the form of society-destroying anarchy that has leveled much of Africa including Rwanda, Somalia, and Liberia where Bandenkreig has included human sacrifice and ritual killing.[2,3] Some children in Rwanda were reduced to picking undigested pieces of corn out of human excrement for food. Mexican revolutions often go through Bandenkreig stages. Bandenkreig also developed during the Thirty Years War that depopulated much of Germany from 1618 to 1648. Bandenkreig is a real possibility in Civil War II.

Although it didn't receive much attention in the press, inhabitants of Serb-besieged Muslim towns in Bosnia ate the flesh of their own dead.[4] The Muslims resorted to cannibalism rather than surrender because surrender to the Serbs meant gang rape and mass murder—not food. In our first civil war, when Vicksburg surrendered, the starving citizens were given food, not raped and murdered. It is clear that Civil War II will be more like the war in the former Yugoslavia than our first civil war because of the intense ethnic hatred that will fuel it. As in Yugoslavia, food will be used as a weapon in Civil War II. I mention these hideous facts not to be sensational, but as a sober lesson of what America will come to when Civil War II sweeps across it.

The Front

The most likely scenario is that America will be split into three new ethnically based nations—a Hispanic southwest, a black south, and a white North. Life in the border areas will not be boring. After the initial chaotic fighting stabilizes, a sort of World War I situation will take hold. The front line

---

2 *The New York Times*, September 1, 1995, p. 1.
3 *The New York Times*, May 9, 1995, p. 4.
4 Hans Askenasy, *Cannibalism*, Prometheus Books, 1994, p. 41.

will most likely run all across the former America, East to West, separating white America from the Hispanic southwest and the black South. A North-South front separating the Hispanics from the blacks is also probable.

What follows describes one possible variation of the front. Many factors, such as the number of artillery pieces available, ammunition resupply, and a host of other political, military, and economic factors will almost certainly make the actual front less devastating than the hypothetical front described below. Still, bear in mind that in certain places and for limited times the actual front will resemble this worst possible front. In fact, in some instances it will likely be much worse. There are no technical reasons why it cannot be so.

The front will have two main features. The first will be the no man's land, an abandoned area between the forward most trench and bunker lines of the opposing sides just as in World War I. The second feature will be an active military zone on both sides of the no man's land extending from the front line back about as far as the enemy's artillery can reach.

Nomans land will vary in width according to circumstances. In flat, deforested land such as deserts it will usually be wider, say 5 miles, about the maximum effective range of light mortars. When the front runs through cities, no man's land is generally at its narrowest, often no more than about 100 yards. During the battle of Stalingrad, no man's land in some cases constricted to the thickness of a wall. In some contested buildings, German and Russian soldiers were separated by nothing more than an interior wall.

I expect automatic cannon to have an impact on the dimension of no man's land similar to that of machine guns during the First World War, and mortars will also have much impact on the dimensions of the future no man's land. The effective combat range of 20mm cannon is just over a mile, and mortars 5 miles. Therefore, we shall assign a width of 1 to 5 miles to the future no man's land. Currently, the heaviest common artillery has a range of about 30 thousand meters or

19 miles, which will determine the width of the military zone on both sides of the front. Therefore, 19 miles for the two military zones times 2 = 38 miles. (I omit the width of no man's land to simplify calculations.)

The total length of this front will be in excess of the approximately 3,000 miles east to west dimension of the current United States. Actually, it will be longer when you allow for its twists and turns, plus the length of the north-south front separating the black south from the Hispanic southwest, and the fronts surrounding besieged cities and enclaves. However, for our purposes we shall use the conservative 3,000 mile figure. A width of 38 miles times a total distance of 3,000 miles equals a total area of 114,000 square miles. If you multiply this figure by the average population density of the current continental United States, 86 persons per square mile, you get an approximation of how many people will be living, but not for long, on this future artillery range— 9,834,699 people.[5]

The point of these computations is to give some idea of the impact of this vast artillery range that will slice up America—the front. All the people living in the front will be displaced—displaced because they will be subject to intermittent artillery bombardment. To put a human face on these numbers, consider that this artillery range is about the same size in area and population as the states of Kentucky, Louisiana, and West Virginia all combined.

Now consider the economic impact that the appearance of this front will have. It is clear that if the above three states were turned into artillery ranges today, it would plunge America into a severe recession. About 10 million people would be displaced and become refugees, and all the production of the factories and farms of these states would be lost—either destroyed outright or completely idle, as there

---

5 Actually, there will be more; these are the 1990 census figures.

would be no workers to operate them. Now consider that all railroads, power lines, highways, and various pipelines crossing the front will be cut. Operation and transport costs for all businesses will soar.

The front will be an apocalyptic landscape of smashed buildings, burnt houses, downed bridges, and cut power lines. Weeds will overgrow all. Former pet dogs now abandoned and feral will roam in packs, many of them rabid. Clouds of mosquitoes will breed in numerous shell holes. Bleached human bones covered with shards of cloth will be seen here and there. And at places there will be mass graves, all unmarked, and most quickly forgotten after the soldiers that filled them are likewise killed.

As a prudent mental exercise, every reader of this book should consider his proximity to this future front. If Civil War II started tomorrow, my home in Northwest New Jersey, for example, would be within artillery range of Dover, New Jersey, which might very well be under the control of Hispanic militias. Where would they get this artillery? Well, there are a number of national guard armories and federal military reserve armories in the greater New York area that do have tanks and artillery pieces stored on their premises; that's where they'll get them. In addition, they might succeed in capturing some of the large U.S. Navy vessels that frequently dock in New York's harbors. And they might receive them from foreign governments sympathetic to their cause.

The Four Phases of Civil War II

We are, in fact, currently witnessing the initial skirmishes of Civil War II because crime bordering on anarchy and racial violence have grown to such extents that they are achieving warlike dimensions. Based on recent history and projections of current trends, I've broken Civil War II into four phases. These four phases are meant to provide a framework for viewing past and current events from the Civil War II perspective, and for understanding future events as they unfold. Still, it should be kept in mind that (unless otherwise noted) when I refer to Civil War II, I'm referring to the all-out and continuous phase of Civil War II when tanks will be rolling down the streets and militias will be shelling cities. This all-out and continuous phase will be the final phase with three preceding phases, the second of which we are now in.

Phase 1—The Foundational Phase

This Foundational Phase began with the cold war, which marked the beginning of our permanent militarization. It shifted into high gear about the mid-sixties, and most of the essential features were in place by the late seventies. This phase ended with the sudden shrinkage of the Russian Empire when the Berlin Wall came down in 1989. This phase was characterized not so much by the establishment resorting to force, but by their emphasizing the mass media to change our concept of ourselves and our nation. During this phase, potent forces were set in motion whose ultimate design was, and remains, imperial conversion. The strategy was essentially twofold—first to break the power of the working class—especially the military potential of the working-class whites—and secondly to so fortify the domination of the international establishment that their grip could never be loosened. This foundational phase of Civil War II was characterized by:

1: Tribalization, or the undermining of the concept of citizenship and its gradual replacement with an imperial tiering system in order to divide the working class along tribal lines.

2: The creeping loss of democracy by shifting real power away from elected officials and to non-elected judges, other appointed officials, private and governmental institutions, and international bodies.

3: Gradually falling wages starting about 1972, and increased wealth for the property-owning class.

4: The slow decay of physical infrastructure of the cities, their abandonment by whites, and their replacement by minorities wedded to the establishment by welfare and affirmative action.

5: Growing legal and illegal immigration to transform America into a typical third-world nation with a poverty-stricken and apathetic peasantry, and to reduce the white percentage of the population.

6: The first appearance of racial associations in police, and the militarization of the police.

7: The creation of a vast international infrastructure of treaties and bureaucrats, many with diplomatic immunity, as part of the imperial tiering system and New World Order.

8: A massive publicity drive to call for gun control in the name of law and order, but whose real purpose was to directly cripple the military potential of the working class, especially the working-class and middle-class whites.

9: The appearance of massive street gangs. While these gangs were not a component of imperial conversion, they are a manifestation of its increasingly successful implementation, and the establishment is now faced with the task of co-opting them or crushing them.

10: The co-option of the mass media, especially the electronic media, to de-emphasize some events and highlight others, all in relation to their impact on imperial conversion.

Phase 2—The Terrorist Phase

This Terrorist Phase, the one we are currently in, will probably last between another five to twenty years. The key to the end of this phase is the coming chaos in Mexico and the ongoing demographic transformation of our Southwest. This phase is characterized by significant and increasing violence by both the imperial security forces and the resistance. During this phase, the antiestablishment violence is typically carried out by individuals and small groups of part-time radicals with little support from the increasingly disaffected but still mainly complacent majority. This current Terrorist Phase of Civil War II is characterized by:

1: The acceleration of Foundational Phase trends such as tribalization, imperial conversion, and the conversion of America into a third-world nation.

2: Increasingly frequent tribal riots, some featuring multiple day extension, barricades, and heavy weapons.

3: Increasing formation of ethnic militias, armed cults and gangs.

4: Increasing talk of secession and a second civil war by both the establishment, and antiestablishment groups and individuals.

5: Increasing commonness of terrorist bombings, sabotage and other acts of violence against the government.

6: A steady rise of tribal violence as individuals and small groups increasingly attack persons of other ethnic groups.

7: Small scale ethnic cleansing as merchants, homeowners and others are driven out of areas in which they are not the race of a majority of the inhabitants.

8: The demographic and political Reconquista of our southwest. Mexican politicians will call for the return of "their" Southwest. Massive Mexican immigration into the southwest and white flight out of it will transform the southwest into a *de facto* province of Mexico. The establishment will surrender much sovereignty of the southwest by treaties, affirmative action, acquiescence to dual citizenship, bilingualism and other devices.

9: The first food riots in cities as government attempts to shut off welfare. The cities and suburbs will begin to divide into ethnic enclaves with walls, gates and guards. Riots will menace the Congress and the White House in Washington D.C..

10: The fragmenting and politicizing of the military. Covert and overt racial factions will become common. Our military will come to resemble the old Soviet military as affirmative action officers politicize it by purging conservative whites and promoting minorities and radical whites. The military's racial composition will shift to mostly minority, especially that portion of the military that conducts ground operations—the Army and Marines because these two branches are vital to actually controlling America. The military will increase operations that give it experience in operating governments, such as the operations in Haiti, Bosnia, and Somalia. Such operations will desensitize the military to the eventual military takeover of the United States of America—the true, ultimate and only real point of all these takeovers of foreign countries.

11: The splitting of many of American groups and institutions along ethnic lines, perhaps even political parties.

12: The abandonment of some areas of our cities by the police to gangs and other armed, non-government groups. White police will be purged from urban forces, and the first firefights will occur between police of different ethnic groups.

13: Gangs beginning to assume political goals and becoming a serious threat to the police in numbers and small arms. Politicians will begin to bid for their military backing. Gangs will begin to take on the characteristics of armies by wearing uniforms, assuming military ranks, standardizing weapons and even acquiring military-style medium and heavy weapons . Gangs will begin to infiltrate military, police and government. The use of armored vehicles and helicopters in anti-gang assaults will no longer be rare, and first use of heavy weapons against gangs will occur in this phase.

14: The first cracks appearing in the loyalty of the white working class to the establishment as imperial conversion and third-world conversion become too obvious to deny.

15: The first armored vehicle being destroyed by the resistance or gangs. A child will be photographed scrounging for food in a garbage dump on American soil.

Phase 3—The Guerrilla Warfare Phase:

This phase will be characterized by the appearance of larger groups of heavily-armed and full-time urban and rural guerillas not unlike like the IRA and the Viet Cong. The establishment will reply with an MVD Internal Security-type force, and massive suspension of civil liberties. Other features of this phase will be:

1: The establishment will acquiesce to gang and militia control of some areas which are entirely (but unofficially) abandoned by the police or the military. The establishment will endeavor to co-opt some gangs and militias by making them de facto security forces, and the federal security forces will mount outright military search and destroy assaults against those who don't disband or cooperate. The military and police will patrol occupied ghettos and other areas with armored vehicles, something like Northern Ireland. The use of heavy weapons by both sides will be common.

2: Mexico will enter a period of chaos, civil war, and starvation. Cross-border guerrilla raids from Mexico will occur, some with the support of the Mexican government. Full-time guerrilla bands will appear in the southwest and other areas.

3: Radical and ethnically-oriented parties will win local and even state elections.

4: Car and truck bombs will become common. Assassinations of police officers and minor politicians will become common.

5: Multiple-day tribal riots with barricades and sieges of police stations will become common.

6: Gangs will become primarily political in their goals and shift into a paramilitary mode.

7: The first instances of medium-scale ethnic cleansing will occur.

8: There will be mutinies in the military, firefights for control of military bases, and the conversion of military bases into firebases will begin. A Soviet-style federal internal security force with heavy weapons will be created to quash riots, break strikes, track-down guerrillas, smash mutinies by the police and military, and to battle urban gangs grown into armies. Firefights between police of different ethnic groups and towns will become common.

9: A general and nationwide flight of persons out of areas in which their ethnic group is not in the majority will occur. *De facto* secession will occur as cities and suburbs seal off adjacent areas of different ethnic composition with walls. A more or less permanent state of recession will set in. Defeat in a foreign war becomes probable as the international power balance shifts against American interests. Massive flight into walled suburbs and villages will occur.

10: The capital will be removed from Washington D.C. to a more secure area.

11: All remaining features of The Bill of Rights will be suspended, certainly in effect, perhaps even overtly by decree. The military will take over much of the USA in much the same manner as they took over many foreign countries like Somalia.

This guerrilla phase will be shorter than the current terrorist phase as events will take on a snowballing nature and reinforce each other. This phase should last between 10 and 20 years. Its end will be signaled by a total collapse of central authority as America shatters in the convulsions of Civil War II.

Phase 4: All-Out, Continuous Warfare

This phase will be marked by multiple-day riots that the federal military can not crush in all cases. The front will appear. Radicals or a mutinous military will seize the federal government, but this will be a temporary affair as America itself will vanish. States will secede from the Union. There will be a war with Mexico. Large scale food shortages will occur, and even starvation as a global depression takes hold. Massive ethnic cleansing will occur as new nations emerge. Occupation by UN troops is a possibility. Concentration camps, rape camps, and even death camps will appear as war becomes total. Eventually, the war will subside as the new nations fix their boundaries according to the military reality. Peace and new boundaries are formalized by treaty—the war will end.

Our society has become so fragile that it can no longer withstand the shocks that it withstood in the past such as war, depression, revolution in Mexico, and lack of relief for the unemployed. If these calamities should ever again test America all at once, America will surely topple into Civil War II.

Civil War II will be preceded by a wave of urban riots that will last an entire summer and extend all across America in every major city. Make no mistake about it, the Los Angeles riot of '92 was Civil War II knocking on the door. Eventually, Civil War II will claw through the door and be upon us like a reptilian predator. These herald riots will be similar to the Los Angeles riot of '92 in that they will last for multiple days before the police and military assemble sufficient force to put them down, and there will be massive looting and burning of entire districts.

The first stage of this summer of riots will seem to be nothing more than the Los Angeles riot of '92 multiplied by most major cities. In this stage, it will still be possible to pretend that the crisis is manageable and temporary like Phase 3 riots. The riots will then shift into a decided military mode. Street gangs and minority militias will set up barricades, lay siege to police stations, take over television stations, capture entire cities, raise revolutionary flags, and demand negotiations with the federal government for financial relief of the cities, and redress of "racist injustices."

The federal government will appease and beg at exactly the moment when strong leadership is required, and all America will see it. Halfhearted attempts to take back some of the cities will be made. Some will succeed, but some will be stopped, and others totally crushed. Surrendering national guardsmen, soldiers and marines will be paraded on rebel TV for all America and all the world to see. Some mostly minority military units will mutiny and go over to the rebels *en masse*. This will be the point of no return, although many will yet deny it. The rebels will thus acquire sufficient heavy weapons to sustain their endeavors. Throughout the south and southwest, many towns of blacks and Hispanics will declare in favor of the rebellion, and tense standoffs will develop with neighboring white towns.

The President will declare a state of emergency and mobilize every military resource to crush the rebellion. Heavy weapons will be liberally used in street fighting, and many minority civilians will be killed in retaking the few cities that are retaken. Most rebel cities will hold on, defended by massive but unorganized minority militias, street gangs turned into armies, rebel police departments, and rebellious, minority-dominated military units. All remaining military units will divide along ethnic lines. Firefights will erupt on every federal military base, and some, perhaps most, will fall to rebellious, minority-dominated units. General ethnic warfare will erupt all across America where groups are intermingled, and where *de facto* racial enclaves border each other. Now all will know that the point of no return has been passed. America will career toward total tribal war at 120 miles per hour with the Devil in the driver's seat.

Ethnic militias will spontaneously form all across America. Ethnic cleansing will erupt, and isolated pockets of this and that ethnic group will be butchered and bulldozed into mass graves. Cities will be taken under siege, and heavy artillery will be used in their unrestricted shelling. Checkpoints manned by militiamen will appear on all major roads. The economy will go into a crash and burn tailspin. Food will become increasingly scarce at any price, and Americans will fight over garbage they would previously have hesitated to throw to their dog. The militias and gangs, which will now vastly outnumber the police and military, will control black markets, thus increasing both their financial and political clout. The front will appear. The fighting will be chaotic, with collapsing and shifting front lines.

Beyond this stage, little is certain, much is possible, and certain turns of events more likely than others. Mexico will certainly be swept into the vortex. Hostilities in America will precipitate an utter collapse of the Mexican economy, although turmoil in Mexico is likely to precede our own revolution. In either case, the Mexican economy will be devastated, and many Mexicans will fight on American soil. Any Mexican government of any political persuasion that does not assist Mexican ethnics in America will fall and be replaced by one that will. Mexican guerrillas will raid the southwest. The American government may be replaced by a military *coup d'etat* or elected radicals. During this initial and chaotic stage of all-out warfare, America will be divided into at least three new ethnically-based regions. All old power structures will be thrown down or greatly modified. The next stage (stage 2) will be one of military deadlock as front lines stabilize. This second stage deadlock of all-out warfare will be caused by the lack of political and military centralization in the three new regions. After considerable turmoil including fighting within each region, centralization will be achieved in each new nation to one degree or another. Thereafter, each will turn its attention to mobilizing all its assets to the escalation of the war.

Stage 3 of the all-out war phase will see the military ascendancy of one side, or an alliance of two sides, and the establishment of a new order in North America, based on the degree of the military victory achieved. Probably all three new nations will survive, but ethnic cleansing to the point of absolute genocide can not be dismissed as a real possibility.

This is the admittedly theoretical blueprint for Civil War II in imperial America. Doubtless, the real war will differ markedly, but will just as surely adhere to this scenario in many of its features. Technically viewed, we are now in the second of the four phases of Civil War II. Our first Civil War had such preceeding phases characterized by slave revolts, angry talk of secession, guerrilla warfare in Kansas, terrorist actions like John Brown's raid on Harpers Ferry, assaults on abolitionists, political realignments, and a general hardening of opinion. Watch for more events that demonstrate our current pre-military phases resemble the pre-military phases of Civil War I. And watch for increasing mentions of this resemblance in the media.

Ethnic Enclaves: Fortresses or Death Traps ?

"A racially-integrated community is a chronological term timed from the entrance of the first black family to the exit of the last white family."—Saul Alinsky

Every reader of this book should consider his own local situation. Are you living in an enclave that can be easily surrounded and cut off from outside help, like Dawson and Forsyth counties to the north of Atlanta? If you are, you're likely a statistic, history, gone with the wind. Well, your local militia might be able to hold them off till the federal cavalry comes galloping to your rescue. Then again, they'll more likely be ambushed and cut to pieces on Route 19 before you can even hear their bugle call. And of course, you have to consider that the federal cavalry might be too busy up north to bother with you. And you even have to consider that the federal cavalry might have every intention of coming to do you harm. It did happen that way in a previous war in your area. Remember? You might consider surrendering, in which case you will have to explain to some besieging militia commander, whose name will likely be something like General Abdullah Mohammed, why your great, great, great, great grandfather raped his great, great, great, great grandmother. Be advised it will not be a good idea to point out to him that that makes you cousins. It is not likely he'll perceive either kinship or humor in your reply. The most probable case is that surrendering will be, to put it delicately, an ill-advised exercise in self-deception.

Consider all the pertinent facts of your local area. Make some approximation, however crude, of how the military situation will develop locally. What National Guard armories and federal military bases are nearby? What heavy weapons are stored there? What is the ethnic mix of the personnel stationed there? How vulnerable are these military bases to siege? Are there militias or gangs active in your area? What are their numbers, armaments, political, and ethnic loyalties?

Is your area a surrounded ethnic enclave? If so, consider this: For an enclave to be economically viable, it must have secure sources of food, fuel, water and electricity. If these are not internal to the enclave, they must be imported from a nearby area securely in the hands of co-ethnics, and that means that corridors for these essential items must be punched through hostile territory by military force and kept open by military force.

All essential roads, power lines, water and fuel pipelines must be identified and their military vulnerability analyzed. If this military opening of corridors can not be accomplished and sustained, then your enclave is not viable. And keep in mind that offensive operations to force open and keep open these corridors in actual combat conditions will be infinitely more difficult than planning such operations on paper in peacetime. Additionally, prudent individuals should acquire knowledge of the military assets and military potential of neighboring ethnic enclaves composed of ethnic groups other than theirs.

While the focus should be on self-defense, in objective terms self-defense may, as circumstances evolve, necessitate offensive operations. At that point, preemptive strikes must be allocated a priority consistent only with their calculated utility. It must be pointed out that during Civil War II ethical restraints will undergo modification to the point of inversion.

What is the ethnic pattern in your area? Is it changing, and how? Make an objective projection of what it will be five, ten, twenty years from now? Some demographers say that actual experience reveals that once an area becomes one-third black, whites begin a rapid and general exodus, and the area rapidly converts to entirely black.

How far is your home from what will likely be the future location of the front? Specifically, is it within artillery range? If not, consider that areas just outside the military zone will be flooded with refugees. Consider again how economically viable your area will be during Civil War II. There are many locations, such as Las Vegas, Nevada; and Hawaii that will become non-viable, perhaps to the point of mass starvation, as they are dependent on economic patterns that will be disrupted or disappear during the hostilities. Smaller communities in primarily agricultural areas far from the front should suffer relatively less.

To be sure, these considerations will not be of great importance for some time. Although its eruption is certain, it is not likely that Civil War II will commence its all-out and continuous military phase for at least another fifteen years. Still, the impact of Civil War II should be something prudent individuals devise some plan for, just as they plan for other events within the same general time frame, such as retirement and a college education for their children.

If you look at a map depicting ethnic patterns as they exist today (at the county level), you can get some glimpse of how the enclave situation is shaping up.

In southeast Alabama and the central Florida panhandle there is currently a white enclave I'll refer to as the Dothan-Pensacola Enclave. It's more or less the counties of Covington, Coffee, Geneva, Dale, and Houston; and the Florida counties of Santa Rosa, Okaloosa, Walton and Holmes. This enclave appears large enough on a map to be viable, at least initially, and it has the added attraction of possessing an outlet to the sea.

The small and isolated white enclave of Lee County in eastern Alabama looks like it will be an interesting place during Civil War II, but not for long. Evacuate now and avoid

Enclaves in Alabama

the rush. There are five counties in central Alabama I'll call the Birmingham—Montgomery Corridor Enclave, because they lie between these two cities. These counties—Shelby, Bibb, Chilton, Autauga and Elmore—are in the middle of the Black Belt that sweeps across the South, and the blacks in the cities of Birmingham and Montgomery will supply much manpower for the siege of this enclave. It may be feasible to hold open a corridor through Saint Clair County to the white counties North of Birmingham, but this enclave's elongated shape makes it defense manpower-intensive, and this enclave will be outmanned as well. Also, the whites of the Birmingham-Montgomery Corridor Enclave may be peacefully displaced by a growing black population before hostilities commence. Bottom line: In either case, move to the white enclave north of Birmingham.

This white enclave just to the north of Birmingham consists of Franklin, Marion, Winston, Walker, Cullman, Blount, Marshall, Jackson and De Kalb Counties, which I'll call the 278-75 Enclave after the two highways that connect it to Mississippi and Tennessee. This enclave is more defensible, with a greater chance of maintaining links with the white areas of Tennessee. Still, the 278-75 Enclave is vexed by its elongated shape which will stress its defenders' resources. The defenders of this enclave may be able to hold open highway corridors to the white areas of Tennessee. One such corridor would be through Tishomingo County in extreme northeast Mississippi, and the other through their own Jackson County where it meets Marion County in Tennessee.

Enclaves in Tennessee

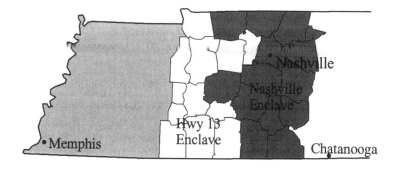

There's an interesting situation developing in western Tennessee. The mainly white counties of Stewart, Benton, Houston, Dickson, Cheatham, Decatur, Perry, Hardin, Wayne, Lewis and Lawrence look as if they're becoming an enclave, which I'll refer to as the Highway 13 Enclave. They may be blocked off from the white area to the east by the following Tennessee counties—Montgomery, Roberston, Sumner, Trousdale, Davidson, Wilson, Hickman, Williamson, Rutherford, Maury, Bedford, Giles, Marshall, and Lincoln. I'll refer to these counties as the Nashville Enclave. If the Nashville Enclave's percentage of blacks continues to grow, the Highway 13 Enclave may loose its viability.

On the other hand, the Nashville Enclave may itself may be surrounded and cutoff from the heart of the Black Belt to the south and east. It's rather like the oriental game of GO, where the object is to maneuver your pieces to surround the enemy's pieces, while he is likewise trying to surround and cut off your pieces.

Further east in Tennessee, the blacks of the Chattanooga Enclave, apparently consisting only of the blacks of Chattanooga, appear to be in an entirely untenable situation. Their small urban enclave is at this time entirely surrounded by whites. The Chattanooga Enclave sets astride the intersections of railroads, the Tennessee River, and several interstate highways essential to the survival of 278-75 Enclave in Alabama and the white counties of Northern Georgia. It will doubtless be a priority objective in Civil War II.

In the former Yugoslavia, road and rail corridors (and the nearby highpoints that gave their possessors military dominance over these corridors) were bitterly contested objectives, even to the point of launching mass infantry assaults that often amounted to little more than suicide to secure them. The future black militia commander of the Chattanooga Enclave will be well advised to reach an accommodation with local white militias, preferably before the fighting breaks out, just as the cut off Moslem enclave of Bihac in Northwest Bosnia reached an accommodation with the besieging Serb militias.

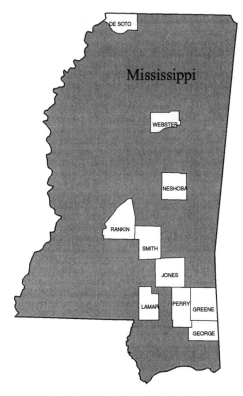

Enclaves in Mississippi

In Mississippi, the whites in De Soto, Webster, Neshoba, Rankin, Smith, Jones, Lamar, Perry, Greene and George counties are all engulfed by the Black Belt, and no serious consideration should be given to their defense when hostilities break out.

Militia commanders should consider requests to aid nearby enclaves of co-ethnics from a purely military perspective, the perspective of triage. The triage system was developed by military medical personnel for treating battle casualties when their numbers do not allow full medical attention to every patient. At that point, all incoming battle wounded are placed into one of three categories. A designated medical *triage* officer with a marker, perhaps a grease pencil, puts a mark on the forehead of each incoming causality. A large "D" means (D)elay, which indicates that the wounded soldier will probably live even if he receives no medical attention at all. They are simply set aside, perhaps with a shot of morphine if they're lucky, and medical treatment is (D)elayed until the triage situation is no longer in force. An "E" mark indicates that the wounded soldier is (E)xpected to die even if he receives prompt and extensive medical attention. These terminal cases are likewise set aside without treatment. An "I" mark means that the wounded soldier falls into the intermediate category - that he will probably live if he receives prompt medical treatment and that he will probably die if he does not. The "I" means (I)mediate, and this triage category of wounded are the only ones that receive immediate and extensive medical attention.

Triage logic is brutal, as is most military theory and military reality, but it cannot be argued with. The whites of Southeastern Mississippi are clearly an "E" enclave, and they should base all expectations and preparations squarely on this big "E" reality. The situation in Georgia is shaping up clearly enough. There's a white enclave in Southeast Georgia I'll call the 341-84 Enclave after two primary highways that intersect in its approximate center at the town of Jesup. The 341-84 Enclave includes the counties of Toombs, Jeff Davis, Appling, Wayne, Long, Bacon, Pierce, Brantley, and Camden. The 341-84 Enclave fits exactly into the "E" category.

Also in the "E" category are the counties of Echols, Berrien, Colquitt, Lee, Taylor, Peach, Pike, Fayette, Columbia, Glascock, Effingham, and Bryan. In northern Georgia, if you draw a line from Forsyth County northeast, and a line from Cherokee County northwest, the area to the north is white. This area is not properly speaking an enclave because it adjoins with white areas in Tennessee and North Carolina. However, the Black Belt may expand north, displacing whites along the Forsyth-Dawson line, and almost the entire area will be within the range of the artillery of black secessionists.

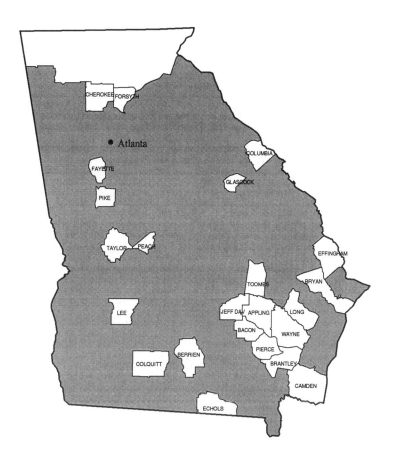

Enclaves in Georgia

From Atlanta, Georgia up the Atlantic seaboard to about Baltimore the pattern is pretty well fixed. The closer to the Ocean and the old Tidewater plantations, the higher the percentage of blacks. Starting at the Appalachians and westward, the population is almost all white. One expects that as geographic segregation increases in the future, both regions will become increasingly monoethnic as whites abandon the

Tidewater area. Where the two areas meet, basically in the Appalachian foothills, the Front will divide the two areas, and much ethnic cleansing will take place. The whites will enjoy a decided military advantage here because they will occupy the high ground all along the Front.

I will make mention of one particular North Carolina county, Dare County. Any white militias in Dare County are whistling Dixie, and they had better select the short version. On a county level demographic map, they're a snow white mini-Rhodesia surrounded by heavily black counties. I suppose Dare County is some sort of enclave for wealthy whites, or else all this is just a misprint on the map. In any case, they're history.

What some presently refer to as the Black Belt will define the new independent black nation. Start at Houston and draw a line along Interstate 45 up to the Dallas—Ft. Worth area. From there the line pretty much follows Interstate 30 up to Little Rock, Arkansas. From Little Rock follow highway 67 to the small town of Newport, Arkansas. From Newport the line runs due east to another small town in Tennessee, Cov-

Breakup of the United States

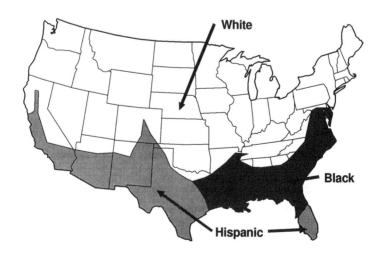

ington. From Covington the line swings around Memphis and then follows highway 78 southeast to Birmingham, Alabama. From Birmingham it follows Interstate 20 to Atlanta. From there just more or less follow the Appalachian foothills up to Baltimore, Maryland, perhaps by following Interstate 85 to Greensboro, North Carolina, and then take Highway 29 the rest of the way to Baltimore. And don't forget to chop off southern Florida. That's hispanic, and the boundary between the black south and hispanic Florida should be Interstate 4.

Those living near the line will dispute its course, saying that it really runs fifty miles thisaway, or umpteen miles thataway of where I drew it. I concede that local residents obviously know more about their area than I do.

This line was drawn based on current demographic patterns and trends. One is the relatively strong demographic trend of blacks returning to the South, and the growing trend of whites vacating heavily black areas in the South. At some point of increasing black population, which many demographers put at one-third of the total population, whites tend to begin to vacate the area, which increases the black portion of the population, which soon precipitates a general abandonment of the area by whites. Also, one must bear in mind the higher birth rate of blacks. The line I drew took these trends into account, and thereby put the line nearer its maximum future value. Depending on when Civil War II actually breaks out, the line may be different.

The Hispanic Southwest

> "Whoever conquers a free town and does not demolish it commits a great error and may expect to be ruined himself."—*Machiavelli*

From Houston, Texas follow Route 45 to Dallas. From Dallas follow highway 287 all the way up to Denver, Colorado. From there follow interstate 25 to Albuquerque, New Mexico. From there follow route 40 to Barstow, California. From there follow highway 58 to Bakersfield, California. From there follow highway 99 through Fresno and on up to

Sacramento. Then follow Route 80 to San Francisco. That's about it, except you also have to throw in the entire Sacramento Valley up to Redding. That's Mexamerica, Aztlan, New Hispania. Call it what you will, that's approximately the land the Hispanics will take back during the Reconquista, according to current demographic patterns.

There are numerous Anglo enclaves in this area, specifically the following Texas counties—Hamilton, Llano, Washington and Fayette. In the Panhandle, there is a possible multiple county enclave consisting of Hartley, Oldham, Randall, Hutchinson, Carson, Armstrong, Gray and Donley counties. In Colorado, Fremont county appears to be shaping up as an enclave for affluent whites who deem themselves too damn good for Denver. In the vast suburb of Southern Cali-

Enclaves in Texas

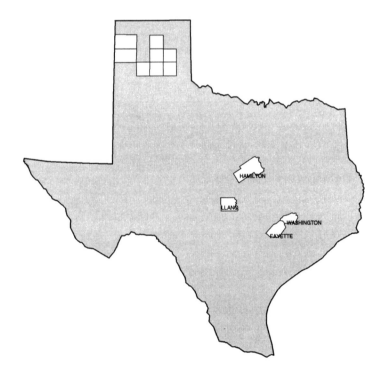

fornia, there will be many Anglo enclaves here and there ... for a while.

The enclave problem may take care of itself to a certain extent. As Civil War II approaches, a great exodus out of surrounded enclaves will take place, causing a collapse of housing values in the Black Belt and the Hispanic Southwest. Many will lose most of the equity in their homes because of this exodus and collapse of housing values. A similar exodus of English-speakers out of Quebec is now taking place. Our exodus will be worse because, unlike the English speakers in Quebec, our enclavers are facing the prospect of butchery. Readers of this book who live in enclaves have fair warning, but they should not tarry in selling out and moving out. Watch for a growing mention of this tribal exodus in the media and real estate business, and its impact on real estate prices. When the media picks up on it, move out immediately or it will be too late. Sell out, move out, stay alive.

Who Thinks America Will Break Up?

"You have plenty of rights in this country, provided you don't get caught exercising them."—Terry Mitchell, Executive Editor, *The Revolutionary Toker*

Most Americans will dismiss the scenario of America breaking up as farfetched, but others have independently developed similar lines of thought. One is Professor Martin van Creveld of the Hebrew University in Jerusalem, Israel. Professor van Creveld is arguably the world's foremost military theorist, and his works receive close attention at West Point and similar institutions worldwide. In his recent book, *The Transformation of War*, Professor van Creveld made many disturbing observations about the chronic instability of multiethnic societies. Here's what Professor van Creveld had to say about America:

"The United States is another large, multi-racial society where weapons are widely available and that has a tradition of internal violence second to none. During most of its history, abundant natural resources, an open frontier, and—later—global expansion enabled Americans to raise their standard of living. As they did so, from time to time they fought a war in which their aggressions found an outlet."

"However, none of these factors any longer exist. The frontier was closed long ago. America's economic viability has been on the decline since about 1970. Partly as a result, so has its ability to dominate the rest of the world, a process that the recent eclipse of the USSR is unlikely to halt. As Americans found it took running faster and faster just to stay in place, social tensions have mounted and so has escapism—the use of drugs; President Reagan described it as 'our number one war.' America's current economic decline must be halted; or else one day the crime that is rampant in the streets of New York and Washington, D.C. may develop into low intensity conflict by coalescing along racial, religious, social, and political lines, and run completely out of control." [1]

There you have it. That's what one of the world's foremost military theorists thinks of our country's future.

Here's another mention of the approaching war. In his book, *The Decline and Fall of the American Empire*, Gore Vidal said this: [2]

> "In due course, something on the order of the ethnic rebellions in the Soviet Union or even of the people's uprising in China will take place here. . . . we are now in a prerevolutionary time. Hence, the emphasis in the media on the breakup of the Soviet Union and Yugoslavia, or of anything other than the breakdown, if not breakup, of the United States and its economy."

Here's another recent mention of Civil War II in America. In a recent controversial book titled *Alien Nation*, Mr. Peter Brimelow maintained that increasing immigration, both legal and illegal, is having many negative impacts on America including more crime, unemployment, environmental impacts, and shifting racial patterns. Here's what Mr. Brimelow had to say:

> "In effect, by allowing its borders to vanish under this vast whirling mass of illegal immigrants, the United States is running on the edge of a demographic buzzsaw. One day, it could suddenly look down to find California or Texas cut off." [3]

Mr. Brimelow also suggested that all illegal aliens in America be rounded up and deported. In the April 1995 issue of *Atlantic Monthly Magazine*, a Mr. Jack Miles reviewed Mr. Brimelow's book, and described what would happen if the

---

1 Martin Van Creveld, *The Transformation of War*, The Free Press, 1991, p. 195.
2 Gore Vidal, *The Decline and Fall of the American Empire*, Odonian Press, 1992, pp. 50, 57.
3 Peter Brimelow, *Alien Nation*, Random House, 1995, p. 35.

federal government tried to roundup and deport all the illegal aliens in Los Angeles.

> "Such an operation could be implemented only at gunpoint, and it would be resisted in the same way. Its announcement would be a virtual declaration of civil war."[4]

What Mr. Miles is saying is that the American government can no longer enforce its own laws on its own soil without igniting a civil war, and that's simple fact. It can't because vast stretches of Southern California are no longer American, but are *de facto* a new nation, exactly as all the southwest will be before 2050 AD. We can't enforce our own laws on our own soil without igniting a civil war; what more proof of societal instability does anyone really need?

Another reference to a second civil war in America occurred in the February 2, 1994 *New York Post* editorial of Patrick Buchanan. Here's what Mr. Buchanan said about the California Civil Rights Initiative, a ballot proposal that would outlaw affirmative action by the state of California.

> "It is about whether we are going to remain one country, or whether there is a Bosnia in our future. . . . from the racial resentments and ethnic hatreds aired daily on radio and TV, it is clear that America is headed towards Balkanization."

It didn't get much attention in the American press, but both the formation of ethnic militias and in-your-face TV and radio shows preceded the outbreak of war in the former Yugoslavia.

Lawrence Hall, in his excellent news column, said this concerning the federal siege of the Montana Freemen.:

> "Clearly, the siege at Jordan represents the beginning of a fight involving brother against brother, and portends to be an uncivil war capable of ripping apart the country."

---

4 *The Atlantic Monthly*, Book Review by Jack Miles, April, 1995, p. 136.

In a recent edition of the *US News and World Report*, John Leo had this to say in an essay entitled "Just Say No to the New Segregation":[5]

"The separatist instinct—even black yearbooks and black parents' associations at integrated schools—should be fought. Those who believe this is one nation and not a large version of the former Yugoslavia ought to start undermining segregation wherever it appears."

Here's a literary version of a second civil war. The April 30, 1995 issue of the *Washington Post* carried a short story by William Lind.[6] Its format was a look back from the year 2050 at a revolution that had swept America just after the turn of the century.

"The triumph of the Recovery was marked most clearly by the burning of the Episcopal Bishop of Maine. She was not a particularly bad bishop. She was, in fact, quite typical of Episcopal bishops of the first quarter of the 21st. Century: agnostic, compulsively political and radical and given to placing a small idol of Isis on the altar when she said the communion service. By 2037, when she was tried for heresy, convicted and burned, she had outlived her era."

"It's funny how clearly the American century is marked: 1865 to 1965. The First Civil War made us one nation. After 1965 and another war, we disunited—deconstructed—with equal speed into blacks, whites, Hispanics, women, gays, victims, oppressors, left-handed albinos; you name it. In three decades we covered the distance that had taken Rome three centuries to cover."

As many others, Mr. Lind has noticed the ongoing transformation of America into a third-world nation. New York has been called "Calcutta on the Hudson" by some.

"By the 1990s the place had the stench of a third-world country. The cities were ravaged by punks, beggars, and bums."

---

5 *US News and World Report*, "Just Say No to Segregation", December 11, 1995, p. 39.
6 *The Washington Post*, "Militant Musings", April 30, 1995, Sect. 3, p. 3.

Mr. Lind story next described how the blacks of Newark, New Jersey declared marshal law in 2009 and began stringing up street criminals. The President sent in the national guard.

"The people of Newark met the troops and begged for their help, and the soldiers either went over or went home. Washington ordered in the 82nd Airborne. The New York Air Guard painted pine tree insignia on its aircraft and threatened to bomb any federal forces approaching Newark. On May 3, Gov. Ephraim Logan of Vermont told the legislature that the federal government no longer represented the people of the state and asked for a vote of secession. Vermont became a republic the next day."

As I do, Mr. Lind draws a contrast between the nature of our first and second civil wars.

"The first Civil War was, on the whole, a gentlemanly affair; the second one wasn't. . . . it was what Lebanon or Yugoslavia saw in the late 20th century."

Mr. Lind also foresees the shelling of cities by artillery, and the revolt in the southwest, with the same results.

"The Reconquista drove the Anglos out of Texas, New Mexico, Arizona and Southern California; the Anglos drove the Hispanics out of what was left of the American West. Blacks and Hispanics in L.A. turned on each other, but there were a lot more Hispanics. Korean Marines landed in Long Beach to get their people out."
"The Deep Greeners took over Oregon .... If you weren't one of them, you didn't get a breathing license, and they tied a plastic bag over your head."

After the "Deep Greeners" are overthrown, Japan takes over the Northwest and gives the people representation in the Japanese Diet. Northern California winds up as the "Azanian Republic."

"It made Oregon look rational by comparison. The Azanian government in Berkley was, in its final incarnation, run by a coalition of radical feminists, Maoist guerrillas and militant vegetarians. The only crime was eating meat. The end came after Azania was overrun by animals who, by law, could be neither killed nor eaten."

Mr. Lind has a "second Confederacy" established by 2017 in the old South, except for southern Florida. I'm on record as giving the advantage to southern blacks. However, I'll allow that the demographic transformation is not yet much advanced in the South. If a hispanic revolt in the southwest touches off ethnic warfare in the south before blacks and poverty drive most whites out (say, about Mr. Lind's 2017), then a second Confederacy seems the better wager.

Canada breaks up and parts of it join our New England states in a new country called Victoria, modeled after the Victorian era of Britain. *McGuffy's Reader* becomes the standard school text, lawyers are set to work digging potatoes, and criminals who "mugged on Tuesday are hung on Wednesday." Mr. Lind calls this deliberate remake of society to conform to an earlier era "retroculture." Mr. Lind has a point in this prediction. In times of stress, people tend to become strongly tribal and religious. People flock to fighting ideologies, or convert current belief systems into fighting ideologies.

Mr. Lind ends on an optimistic note. Eventually, things settle down except in the southwest where the armies of "Nueva Espana" are fighting the Indian "Aztec Alliance."

Mr. Lind is a noted military writer, was an advisor to presidential candidate Gary Hart, and is currently the director of the Free Congress Foundation. One does have to admit that the truth does have a nasty habit of unfolding as stranger than fiction, and Mr. Lind's projections (and mine!) may pale when when held up against the actual Civil War II which is just around the corner.

This is from an article by former Secretary of State, Lawrence Eagleburger, which appeared in the March, 1996 *National Times*:

> "Meanwhile, the global process of decentralization proceeds, what is happening in Bosnia; in Khazia; Spain with their Basques; in the UK with the Scots; is a tendency toward minimalist nationalism. . . . This process is happening in the U.S. as well."

Here's a sign that the military is not unaware of the growing unrest in America. In an article in the January *Atlantic Monthly*, an article by Thomas E. Ricks reported that Air Force Col. Charles Dunlap had written a remarkable essay whose subject was a military *coup d'etat* in America. The title: "The origins of the American Military Coup of 2012." I quote the beginning of the article:

> "It is the year 2012. The American military has carried out a successful *coup d'etat*. Jailed and awaiting execution for resistance to the *coup*, a retired military officer writes to an old comrade, explaining how the *coup* came about."

The article notes this remarkable treatise was entered in the National Defense University's Chairman of the Joint Chiefs of Staff Strategy Essay Competition, and that it essay was selected as co-winner of said competition. Most remarkable of all, its author, Col. Dunlap, was honored by Gen. Colin Powell at the awards ceremony.

And here's another tremor from the military. In the January, 1996 *Progressive*, Peter Cassidy, in an article entitled "Guess Who's the Enemy",[7] quoted an Army publication named *Tomorrow's Missions*. In this publication, Lieutenant General J.H. Binford Peay III asserted that in the Army of the 1990s:

> "Military forces are required to provide domestic national assistance, such as internal peacekeeping and antidrug operations and support of civil authorities to maintain stability in a rapidly changing America."

Here's yet another indication that our military is being recast as a Soviet-style MVD Internal Security force. The Green Panthers are a secessionist group advocating an Independent "Stoners Homeland" in the Pacific Northwest for marijuana users. Their publication, *The Revolutionary Toker*,

---

7 *The Progressive*, "Guess Who's the Enemy", January, 1996, p. 22.

had an article titled, "The Calm Before The Storm Troopers".[8] The article concerned Gen. Barry McCaffrey (US Army Ret.) who was made the head of the Office of National Drug Control Policy. The article contained this unsettling information about Gen. McCaffrey:

> "His doctoral thesis at the Army War College, Use of Standard Operational Planning to Quell Domestic Civil Disturbances, won him his third star. In his thesis he applies various military scenarios within cities to suppress civil unrest."

Note that the much-promoted "war on drugs" provides an expedient vehicle for the establishment to desensitize the military to domestic operations, and to bring up the military's heavy firepower for the inevitable showdown with the urban gangs as they accelerate their ongoing transformation into political/military organizations. The establishment must at all costs retain its monopoly on political and military power to realize its ultimate goal, imperial conversion, and this will ultimately require turning the military's heavy firepower on any and all who oppose that goal and monopoly.

Here's another mention of civil war in America. The Nov. 12, 1995 issue of the *Boston Globe* magazine had an article written by John Powers, an article titled "The Splintering of America".[9] The article cited the usual ethnic and linguistic mess that America has become and openly asked:

> "Is the United States destined to come apart as the Soviet Union did, fracturing into dozens of rival sociocultural and political enclaves?"

---

8 *The Revolutionary Toker*, Vol. 6, No. 2. (1996). The Green Panther's address is PO Box 31231, Cincinnati, OH 45231, phone (513)522-6264.

9 *The Boston Globe Magazine*, "Splintering of America", Nov. 12, 1995, p. 23.

At the end of the article, where writers usually sum up their point, a professor of ethnic studies at the University of California, Berkley, Ronald Takaki, was quoted as saying:

> "We have a double vision. We look at our diversity, and we also look at Bosnia—and we worry."

The overall tendency is for establishment types to predict a crime and poverty-stricken multiracial banana republic, something like Brazil. Brazil is wracked by violence, but has so far avoided massive bloodshed like Bosnia. In such a society, the establishment reckons it can endure quite nicely behind its razor wire, walls and security guards. This optimistic view is based on their utter contempt for working-class whites. I'm confident they will be proven wrong, but time will tell.

This is from an essay by Charles Krauthammer in the November 13, 1995 issue of *Time* magazine:

> "America is proceeding blithely down the path of diversity and ethnic separatism. America's destination, however, is not Canada, which will find some civil way out of its dilemma. America's destination is the Balkans."[10]

Here's another mention of civil war in America. In the April 10, 1995 issue of *Forbes* magazine, Dr. Thomas Sowell, in an article on affirmative action, said this:

> "Nor do Americans need to go to the brink of civil war before repealing a policy that has produced polarization and intergroup violence in other countries, including even civil war in Sri Lanka."[11]

Here's another mention of a second civil war in America. In the July 19, 1995 issue of *The New York Post*, columnist Scott McConnell had much to say on this subject in a column entitled, "American Apocalypse—Soon?":

---

10 *Time Magazine*, "Quebec and the Death of Diversity", November 13, 1995, p. 124.
11 *Forbes Magazine*, "The 'Q' Word", April 10, 1995, p. 61.

"Civil strife is painful; civil war dreadful beyond words. In its current direction, however, the United States—aggressively multicultural, libertine and violent in its mass entertainment, with its rapidly expanding third-world populations and its corporations eager to pull up stakes and transfer jobs abroad—hardly seems stable in the long run."[12]

Here's what Robert Kaplan had to say in the February, 1994 issue of the *Atlantic Monthly* in an article entitled, " The Coming Anarchy":

"Indeed, it is not clear that the United States will survive the next century in exactly its present form. Because America is a multiethnic society, the nation-state has always been more fragile here than it is in more homogeneous societies like Germany and Japan."[13]

Readers will note that despite all the direct and indirect references to ethnic instability and even ethnic warfare in America, one almost never comes across a simple declarative sentence something like this: " It is probable that America will erupt in ethnic warfare." Simple, right?

Even the timid establishment press has started to admit the inevitability of a second civil war in America, as the above excerpts testify. Collectively, they covered most of the main points: a multiethnic society—a history of extreme internal and external violence—plenty of guns—a sinking economy—waning global power—drug gangs—urban decay—lower wages each year—massive illegal immigration—corrupt politicians—our deliberate transformation into a third-world country—the growing gap between rich and poor—the formation of militias—the rejection of assimilation—and racist affirmative action.

---

12 *The New York Post*, "American Apocalypse—Soon?", Editorial Section, July 19, 1995.
13 *The Atlantic Monthly*, "The Coming Anarchy", Feb., 1994, p. 76.

It is instructive to note that the most explicit, accurate, clinical and extensive of these observations were made by a foreigner, Professor van Creveld. Americans, especially establishment white Americans, cringe when anyone mentions the possibility of a race war in America. They do so partly out of the absurd notion that anyone who breaches the topic must be a racist who desires such a conflict. By the same absurd logic, weathermen must somehow generate the hurricanes they predict.

There is another unspoken reason why even the mention of this topic, or rather its explicit public mention, draws such negative reactions. The establishment, in order to manipulate public opinion, has succeeded in reducing discussions of race relations to a ritual, a ritual for which the high priests of the media and political elite have written the ceremonial script. Nothing outside the ceremonial script is tolerated; all else is heresy. The establishment has succeeded in manipulating the minds of most Americans to the point that racism means white racism exclusively. Black racism simply does not exist in establishment mythology, and any assertion that it does is immediately denounced by shrill accusations of racism. In fact, by the concoction of the racist euphemism affirmative action, the establishment has succeeded in painting black racism as beautiful, rather like putting a dress on a pig.

Despite the establishment's attempts to choke off debate, increasing and organized violence will eventually push the topic onto every television screen and newspaper editorial in America. Watch for more explicit and veiled mentions of Civil War II in the press. As Civil War II draws nearer, they will become more frequent.

In fact, at some point, public endorsement of the possibility of a second civil war in America will become acceptable, even fashionable. Radical blacks will endorse the concept of Civil War II as a means of frightening the largesse out of white liberals and cementing black solidarity. Right-wing whites will also endorse it, some as a projection of what they desire, others because of the chilling signs that it's drawing ever nearer. Some politically-correct whites will embrace it as yet more proof of white racism, and establishment whites will use it as an excuse to increase their power (and therefore the amount of money they can steal.)

Ultimately, the concept of Civil War II will be as much a current topic as, say, the Greenhouse Effect, alternate lifestyles, drugs, or the latest fad diet. One can not fix a problem until one is aware of it. By this measure, the increased talk of Civil War II will be a positive development. The developing trend seems to be that liberal intellectuals think our conversion into an imperial system will be successful, and that a civil war will either not take place or be a sputtering affair easily put down. The conservative commentators seem to be lining up behind the idea that the war will be serious, and that America will probably be partitioned. These two views warrant close monitoring as they are bound to have some impact on the course of events. However, the bottom line is that events will unfold in much the same manner as they did prior to our first civil war. There was much talk of secession and civil war prior to the actual occurrence of both. However, all the talk was sufficient neither to prevent secession, nor even make realistic military preparations for the conflict. Almost all those who foresaw our first civil war imagined it as an almost bloodless summer frolic. President Lincoln asked for 90-day volunteers, and the clueless gentlefolk of Washington packed picnic baskets before heading off to take in the First Battle of Bull Run. (OK, Manassas for you unreconstructed Rebs.)

Nothing indicates that our second civil war will develop any differently. Even those who eventually concede Civil War II's inevitability will envision it as a summer of riots put down by the national guard, and its underlying causes permanently uprooted by some anti-poverty programs and midnight basketball. No, the tribal war drums are beating too loudly for that. It will last years, kill millions, and shatter America into starving tribal enclaves.

The Bloody Lessons of Tribal Europe

"Hang your chemistry and electricity. If you want to make a pile of money, invent something that will enable these Europeans to cut each others throats with greater facility."—Advice from an unidentified American businessman in Vienna, Austria to fellow American Hiram Maxim that inspired his invention of the Maxim Gun, the first fully automatic, modern machine gun.

When will Civil War II actually erupt? There is no scientific formula or mathematical equation that will give us the date. Instead, we must turn our attention to the demographic forces propelling us toward Civil War II, our ongoing transformation from a stable monoethnic nation into an unstable multiethnic empire. Not all history can be explained by this single engine of demographic transformation. Other factors can and do decide the boundaries and fates of empires and nations. However, the concept of nationality has been the dominate historical factor, at least since the industrial revolution. The more monoethnic a nation is, the less chance a secondary tribe will break off and form a new nation, or unite with their co-ethnics in an adjacent nation. The more monoethnic a nation is, the less likely a neighboring country will try to carve off a slice inhabited by its co-ethnics as Nazi Germany seized the Sudentenland of Czechoslovakia. The more monoethnic a nation is, the more likely its citizens will unite and fight foreign invaders, thus again increasing the chances of territorial integrity.

To be sure, ethnic tensions and even genocide can and do occur in relatively monoethnic nations, such as the genocide of the Jews and others in Germany. However, it is the internal stability and territorial integrity of nations that is the focus of our concern. The more usual case is that a secondary tribe dominant in one region breaks off and forms a new nation. Nationalism (tribalism, if you please) is the relentless historical force that has shaped the current map of Europe. The tread of imperial armies has also changed the map of Europe, but empires are like great ships—when sunk they remain sunk. Tribal-based nations, on the other hand, are historically buoyant—pushed under they resurface time and time again.

This view of history requires no elaborate intellectual defense. Consider world maps. They depict the world as their makers perceive it. All the globe (excepting the uninhabited oceans and the uninhabited polar icecaps) is literally divided up and colored as this nation or that. Nationality is plainly what we consider of greatest significance when we perceive our world, not the watersheds of great rivers, vast climatic zones, or ranges of towering mountains. It is not so much the Earth we are mapping, but rather the very synapses of our own minds.

Europe is that ever-troubled region from whence we got our notions of culture, politics, and religion, and is therefore of particular interest to us. Its pattern on the map may as well be lit up in neon lights. The nations of Europe are clearly tribal. Smaller tribes coalesced into super tribes, and nations came into being. The dominant tribe in every nation speaks a common language, usually unique to them, and its members mutually recognize each other as co-nationals.[1]

Consider Table 3a. There are several wars boiling or simmering in Europe. Other European nations are occupied by foreign or UN troops. Some are vassal states of a mightier neighbor. Let's make an objective examination of these troubled countries to see if we can find any common, underlying reason for their misfortunes.

---

1 This chapter was written in the summer of 1995, and reflects the state of Europe at that time.

Nation	Largest Group	Largest %	2nd %	3rd %	Status
Albania	Albanian	96	2		
Armenia	Armenian	90	3	2	Civil War
Austria	Austrian	99	1		
Belarus	Belarussian	78	13	4	
Belgium	Flemish	55	33	1	
Bosnia	Moslem	44	31	17	Civil War
Bulgaria	Bulgarian	85	9	6	
Croatia	Croatian	75	12	1	Civil War
Czech Republic	Czech	94	4		
Denmark	Danish	97	1		
Estonia	Estonia	65	28	3	
Finland	Finnish	94	5	1	
France	French	91	5		Terrorist war
Georgia	Georgian	69	9	7	Civil War
Germany	German	93	2		
Greece	Greek	98	2		
Hungary	Hungarian	96	2	1	
Ireland	Irish	94	3		
Italy	Italian	98			
Latvia	Latvian	52	34	5	
Lithuania	Lithuanian	80	9	7	
Macedonia	Macedonian	67	21	4	UN Occupied
Moldova	Moldovan	64	14	13	Occupied
Netherlands	Dutch	99	1		
Norway	Norwegian	97			
Poland	Polish	98	1	1	
Portugal	Portuguese	99	1		
Romania	Romanian	89	7	2	
Russia	Russian	82	3	3	Civil War
Serbia	Serbian	63	14	6	External War
Slovakia	Slovak	87	11	1	
Slovenia	Slovene	90	3		
Spain	Spanish	73	16	8	Terrorist war
Sweden	Swedish	91	3		
Switzerland	German	74	20	4	
Ukraine	Ukrainian	73	22		
U.K.	English	82	10	2	Guerrilla war

Table 3a: Ethnic composition of European nations.

For the purposes of this analysis of European conflicts, a civil war shall be defined as an active conflict or armed standoff between two armed groups of full-time combatants organized in permanent military formations, each of which controls territory.

A guerrilla war shall be defined as the same as a civil war excepting that the guerrilla formations do not permanently control inhabited territory, but exist in bands continuously on the run or in hiding.

A terrorist war shall be defined as ongoing violence such as riots, bombings, and assassinations, whose perpetrators are not organized in permanent military formations, and who do not control any territory.

Now let's examine the nations that have some sort of conflict listed in the extreme right column of Table 3a.

Armenia:[2] Armenia has been at war since 1989, assisting secessionist Armenian ethnics in the Nagorno-Karabakh region of the neighboring country of Azerbaijan. The Azerbaijani Army was defeated. The secessionist Armenians of the Nagorno-Karabakh have achieved their goal of reunion with Armenia proper, and a tense cease-fire is now in effect—a cease-fire which will last not a second beyond when the Azerbaijanies re-equip their battered army.

Russian ethnics compose 2% of Armenia's population, and they have not been forgotten by Mother Russia. Russian troops are still stationed in Armenia despite Armenia becoming independent in 1990, and Armenia is a now vassal state of Russia. When Russia says frog, Armenia jumps. Armenia's involvement in an external war was caused by ethnic Armenians living outside its borders, and the presence of foreign troops on her soil was caused in part by foreign ethnics residing within Armenia's borders. The underlying cause of Armenia's difficulties is clearly ethnic in nature.

---

2 *Clements International Report*, Political Research, Inc., April, 1995, p. 14.

Bosnia:[3] Bosnia is currently fighting a civil war within its borders against secessionist ethnic Serbs and the usual Serb mass butchery and rape. The civil war in Bosnia is clearly ethnic in nature.

Croatia: Croatia is currently fighting a civil war within its borders against ethnic Serbs who slaughtered and raped Croatians, and then set up their own nation on Croatian soil. The civil war in Croatia is clearly ethnic in nature.

France: France has two terrorist, low-intensity conflicts going on within its borders—one with the Basques and the other on the island of Corsica, legally a part of France. Both conflicts involve unassimilated tribal groups, thus both are ethnic in nature. Both involve groups that are concentrated in one area. Corsica, it should be noted, is an island separate from continental France, much like the relation of the US to Puerto Rico, where we also see ongoing separatist tendencies.

Georgia:[4] Georgia had an ethnically-based civil war in 1992 that still sputters on today. As this chapter was being prepared, persons unknown attempted to kill the leader of Georgia, Eduard A. Shevardnadze, with a car bomb on August 29, 1995. Suspects include followers of the first president of Georgia, a Mr. Gamsakhurdia, who "committed suicide" after he was ousted in a Shevardnadze backed coup. Another suspect is a Mr. Ioseliani, a former bank robber and former ally of Shevardnadze who currently heads up a 5,000 man private army known as the *Mkhedrioni*—Georgian for Knights. A *New York Times* article of Aug. 30, 1995 stated that Georgia "remains a largely lawless, corrupt country dominated by armed gangs." The Times quoted human rights

---

3 *The New York Times*, "An Outlaw in the Balkans is Basking in the Spotlight", Nov. 23, 1993, p. 1.

4 *The Economist*, "How to Make Enemies and Influence People", August 19, 1995, p. 46; *The New York Times*, February 5, 1995, p. 3; *The New York Times*, "Parliament in Georgia Approves Constitution", p. 11.

groups as saying Georgian security forces regularly use "torture and intimidation."

How did Georgia come to this sorry state of *coups*, car bombs, corruption, lawlessness, assassinations, torture, and bank robbers running private armies? When the Soviet Union broke up, Georgia became independent. Almost immediately, two internal minorities, the Abkhazians and the Ossetians, declared independence for their slices of Georgia, and civil war erupted. The Russians intervened in order to look after the interests of 370,000 ethnic Russians in Georgia (7% of Georgia's population), and to generally reduce Georgia to a vassal state. Today, although the civil war sputters on, the rebellious minorities have basically achieved autonomy for their regions, and Russian troops occupy much of Georgia. Georgia is an occupied vassal state of Russia. Georgia's difficulties are clearly ethnic in nature.

Macedonia:[5] Macedonia currently has UN troops stationed within its borders in a symbolic attempt to forestall ethnic conflict. The general opinion has it that civil war between the majority Christian Slavs and the minority Albanian Moslems is not inevitable, but may break out at any time. Macedonia's difficulties are clearly ethnic in nature.

Moldova:[6] Moldova became independent in 1991 when the old USSR broke up. Ethnic Russians residing in the trans-Dniestr region of Moldova seized control of that region in 1992 in a civil war in which 500 died. The ethnic Russians were aided by Russian Cossacks that poured into Moldova, and then Russian troops occupied the trans-Dniestr region of Moldova to protect Russian ethnics living there. Facing impossible odds, in 1994 the Moldovan people voted in a government of former communists that essentially granted autonomy to the Russians of the trans-Dniestr region. The

5 *The New York Times*, April 9, 1995, p. 12.
6 *The New York Times*, Dec. 12, 1993, Sect. I, p. 19; Dec. 27, 1993, p.8; March 1, 1994, p. 8.

trans-Dniestr region of Moldova is currently occupied by Russian troops, and Moldova is a vassal state of Russia that responds as expected when Russia says frog. The civil war in Moldova, its reduction to a vassal state, and its ongoing occupation by foreign troops are difficulties that are clearly ethnic in origin.

Russia: Russia is currently fighting a civil war within its borders against its own nominal citizens who are ethnic Chechens and Moslems. The civil war in Russian is clearly tribal in nature.

Serbia: Serbia is an economically devastated police state that is currently entangled in both internal and external tribal conflicts. Serbia constantly terrorizes its internal minorities (chiefly Moslems). Serbia is also caught up in external ethnic wars. Many Serbian men are fighting covertly in Bosnia and Croatia alongside ethnic Serbs resident in those countries. If no Serbs lived in Bosnia or Croatia, Serbia would not be at war. Serbia is suffering through a devastating UN economic boycott because of its assistance to ethnic Serbs living outside its borders. Serbia is currently home to many psychotic ex-soldiers who have committed unspeakable crimes during the ethnic cleansing campaigns in Croatia and Bosnia. Serbia's problems, however self-inflicted, are clearly tribal in origin.

Spain:[7] Spain is currently fighting a small but nasty secessionist terrorist campaign mounted by one of its minority nationalities, the Basques. It appears that the Spanish security forces have the Basques on the ropes, but be that as it may, the terrorist secessionist campaign in Spain is clearly ethnic in nature.

The United Kingdom: The U.K. is fighting a secessionist movement in Northern Ireland against Irish nationals who seek reunion with Ireland. Currently there is a shaky cease-

---

7　*The New York Times*, "Basques find Inspiration as IRA Talks of Peace", April 16, 1995, p. 6.

fire, punctuated by riots and other unpleasantries. The case can be made that the fighting in Northern Ireland is either a terrorist war or a guerrilla war. In either case, the secessionist campaign in the not so United Kingdom is clearly tribal in nature.

All of these unfortunate countries' problems are mainly or partly ethnic in nature, but that's only half the picture. On Table 3a, these conflicts seem to be randomly distributed because the countries are listed alphabetically.

Now consider Table 3b where the countries are listed by the percentage of the dominant ethnic group. The countries on the uppermost portion of this list are free of serious conflict, but about half the countries of the bottom portion are plagued by war, terrorism, and occupation by foreign armies. The countries at the very top of the list are almost purely monoethnic. They may be rich or poor, or large or small, but they are monoethnic and relatively internally stable. On the other hand, about half the countries on the bottom of the list are multiethnic shooting galleries.

To be accurate, acts of terrorism do occur in the more monoethnic countries of the top of the list. However, these terrorist incidents are usually ethnic in origin as well. Europe's growing third world populations will probably supplant unassimilated European minorities as the most serious terrorist threat in the next century.

The lesson is clear: The more monoethnic a European nation is, the more likely it is to be peaceful and stable. The more multiethnic a European nation is, the more likely it is to experience tribal civil wars. There is simply no real arguing with this brutal fact. The lesson here is that the likelihood of a minority group having a go at a military divorce from the nation increases with its chances of success, and its chances of success increase with its percentage of the population. Consider the most multiethnic nation in Europe—Bosnia. Bosnia was literally born fighting in 1991, and this civil war has produced more dead than any other of the recent wars in Europe. The most multiethnic European nation produced the

Nation	Largest Group	Largest %	2ND %	3RD %	Status
Netherlands	Dutch	99	1		
Portugal	Portuguese	99	1		
Austria	Austrian	99	1		
Greece	Greek	98	2		
Italy	Italian	98			
Poland	Polish	98	1	1	
Norway	Norwegian	97			
Denmark	Danish	97	1		
Albania	Albanian	96	2		
Hungary	Hungarian	96	2	1	
Finland	Finnish	94	5	1	
Czech Republic	Czech	94	4		
Ireland	Irish	94	3		
Germany	German	93	2		
Sweden	Swedish	91	3		
France	French	91	5		Terrorist war
Slovenia	Slovene	90	3		
Armenia	Armenian	90	3	2	Civil War
Romania	Romanian	89	7	2	
Slovakia	Slovak	87	11	1	
Bulgaria	Bulgarian	85	9	6	
U.K.	English	82	10	2	Guerrilla war
Russia	Russian	82	3	3	Civil War
Lithuania	Lithuanian	80	9	7	
Belarus	Belarussian	78	13	4	
Croatia	Croatian	75	12	1	Civil War
Switzerland	German	74	20	4	
Spain	Spanish	73	16	8	Terrorist war
Ukraine	Ukrainian	73	22		
Georgia	Georgian	69	9	7	Civil War
Macedonia	Macedonian	67	21	4	UN Occupied
Estonia	Estonia	65	28	3	
Moldova	Moldovan	64	14	13	Occupied
Serbia	Serbian	63	14	6	External War
Belgium	Flemish	55	33	1	
Latvia	Latvian	52	34	5	
Bosnia	Moslem	44	31	17	Civil War

Table 3b: European nations, arranged by majority percent.

most multiethnic dead. Let me say that again: *The most multiethnic European nation produced the most multiethnic dead.* If there had been only Moslems residing in Bosnia, there would have been no civil war in Bosnia.

Is America a multitribal country and therefore unstable? With each and every passing day, more and more Americans of all ethnic groups are perceiving their tribal affiliation as more self-definitive and more important than their common American nationality. By this measure we are increasingly unstable.

More bad news: Of the European countries, the median size of the most numerous ethnic group is 89%. In America, the most numerous ethnic group (the English-speaking whites) is only 75% of the total population and falling. By this measure, America is again not as internally stable as most European nations. Twelve European nations have primary ethnic groups that are 75% or less of their total population. Seven of these twelve nations are fighting wars, are occupied, or have internal secessionist terrorists.

More bad news: Of the European countries, the median size of the second largest ethnic group is 5%. In America, our second largest ethnic group (the blacks) is 12%. By this measure, America is again not as stable as most European nations. Twelve European nations have secondary ethnic groups that are 12% or more of the total population. Four are fighting wars, two are occupied by foreign troops, one is fighting internal terrorists.

More bad news: Of the European countries, the median size of the third largest ethnic group is 1%. In America, our third largest ethnic group (the Hispanics) is 9%. By this measure, America is again not as stable as most European nations. Two European nations have third ranking ethnic groups that are 9% or more of the population. One is fighting a civil war, the other occupied.

More bad news: In America, 88% of the people speak the most widely-used language (English) as their primary language. Of the European countries, the median size of this percentage is 94%. By this measure, America is again not as stable as most European nations.

More bad news: There are now about six million Moslems in America, and they are expected to outnumber Jews by the end of this decade. America has been described as a Judeo-Christian nation. Are we now to be a Judeo-Christian-Moslem nation and all that that implies? The concept of freedom of religion can absorb only so much cultural diversity. As the Moslem percentage of the population grows, it is predictable that they will demand and eventually get laws allowing polygamy, chopping off the hands of criminals, death by stoning for adulterers, and the host of other antique horrors Moslems embrace. In Miami, Dade County has a special maintenance squad that cleans up dead chickens, goats, lizards, voodoo powder, and other "hex" items found each morning on the grounds of the county courthouse.[8] These items are ritually deposited there by adherents of the Voodoo, Sanataria, and similar religions whose members are appearing before the court on various charges. Almost all are immigrants from the Caribbean islands. Eventually, our diversity will increase to the point that there will be no common basis for our laws. That's why America is becoming an undemocratic imperial system, and that's why we'll break up in a civil war.

In this century in Europe, the core of the old Russian Empire known as the USSR dwindled down to about 50% Russian ethnics and broke up. At the time multi-tribal Yugoslavia exploded in ethnic savagery, its main ethnic group, the Serbs, made up 36% of the population. The multi-tribal Austro-Hungarian Empire broke up after defeat in war. The multitribal British Empire had to give the Irish their freedom after a civil war. Tribal nationalism is clearly the driving force in European politics, and produces the most stable (or if you

---

8 *The New York Times*, August 9, 1995.

prefer, the least unstable) arrangement. What about the other multiethnic countries in Europe, why aren't they embroiled in civil war? Let's take a brief look at them. All the European countries that spun off from the old USSR have Russian minorities: Belarus 13%, Ukarine 22%, Lithuania 9%, Latvia 34%, Estonia 28%. They are relatively peaceful, but live on the lip of the Russian Bear. These countries have achieved stability only by acquiescing to a frog/jump relationship with Russia, and civil war may yet erupt in these unhappy lands.

In our case, can we compare Mexico to Russia, and ourselves to these unfortunate Russian-dominated countries? Both Mexico and Russia are adjacent to the country their co-ethnics reside in. This existence of a common border increases chances of ethnic conflict in three ways: It makes assimilation of the minorities more difficult. It makes further immigration more likely. It makes invasion more feasible.

To be sure, an invasion of America by the Mexican Army would fail militarily, but that's not the point. Remember von Clausewitz: "War is the continuation of politics by other means." Wars are fought to advance the interests of the state. If the interests of the state are immediately secured by initiating the war regardless of the immediate military outcome, then the skeletal hand of the dead Prussian beckons his acolytes towards war. They do have a military academy in Mexico, by the way; and they do not neglect their study of Professor-General von Clausewitz.

The point is that such an invasion of America by Mexico would increase the internal political instability of America, almost certainly to the breaking point. In a very real sense, America exists at the pleasure of Mexico just as surely as the Baltic countries exist at the pleasure of Russia. Mexico can bring down America as surely as Sampson brought down the Philistine Temple.

America's difficulty with the Hispanics in the southwest is similar to Britain's difficulty with the Irish in Northern Ireland. It is instructive to note that America and Britain are the countries in danger of losing their territory, not Mexico or Ireland. Consider this seeming paradox of two major military powers (both of them with nuclear capability!) in danger of losing territory to smaller, poorer, weaker, non-nuclear neighbors. This muscle-bound impotence of America and Britain highlights the inherent weakness of countries that have large internal minorities and a land border with the country of origin of those minorities.

The historic remedies for this malady—if they can be thought of as remedies—are assimilation, ethnic cleansing, institution of a police state . . . or surrender of territory. As for assimilation, the Scots were assimilated into the United Kingdom (read English Empire). The lesson here is that entire groups can be assimilated easier than half a group. With our conquest of Northern Mexico, we foolishly tried to conquer half a people, but the fires of Mexican nationalism burned on in free southern Mexico. They burn still.

What about Belgium and Switzerland? They're multiethnic, more multiethnic than the United States, more multiethnic than many of the European countries with civil wars, yet both are peaceful and prosperous. Belgium (55% Dutch-speaking Flemish, 32% French-speaking Walloons) is peaceful and prosperous, and arguably a more pleasant place to live than America. It wasn't always so. The Dutch-speaking northern half of Belgium and the French-speaking southern Half of Belgium should have been incorporated into Holland and France respectively during the nation building phase that swept Europe during the industrial revolution. For historical difficulties too complex to fall within the scope of this book, Belgium became more or less a buffer state between France and Holland. It came into being in 1830.

It was dominated in all respects by the wealthier French-speaking Walloons of the southern half of Belgium. This dominance of the French gave Belgium a certain stability, but it did not long endure. Slowly, the Dutch grew in relative numbers, political clout and economic power. Ethnic tensions mounted after World War II, culminating in intermittent tribal riots. All three major political parties split into Dutch-speaking and French-speaking wings. The people of Belgium faced the real possibility of civil war, a civil war that would certainly have drawn in both France and Holland.

Wisely, in 1980 constitutional reforms were enacted that recognized four semiautonomous linguistic regions— French-speaking, Dutch-speaking, German-speaking, and a bilingual French/Dutch capital of Brussels. Each region has a sort of legislature or "council" that determines much of what happens in that region. No ethnic group is entirely satisfied with this state of affairs, but it does keep the peace.

Switzerland[9] (65% German, 20% French, 4% Italian) has avoided ethnic conflict, again by the simple expediency of granting much autonomy to its 26 cantons, roughly our equivalents of states, but much more independent. Germans predominate in 17 cantons, the French in 4, and Italians in 1. All but four of the Cantons are unilingual. By and large, each ethnic group remains in its own areas and manages its own affairs.

In most cantons, gun ownership is little restricted, but yet there are no terrorists shooting Swiss policemen in the name of any secessionist movements. Clearly, the Swiss government exists with the full approval of the Swiss people. (Such is not the case in the emerging American empire where private gun ownership is rapidly being rescinded as part of the transformation process as ethnic conflict spreads.)

Multiethnic and multilingual nations can and do work. However, all evidence clearly indicates they work only if each group is allowed to conduct its own affairs without undue meddling by the central government. In Switzerland, the federal government has absolute authority in matters of customs duties and regulations, currency, post and telecommunications, and railways.

---

9 J. Murray Luck, *A Country Study by the Dept. of the Army—History of Switzerland*, The Society for Promotion of Science and Scholarship, 1985.

The cantons have absolute authority in matters concerning police protection, social services, housing and religion. In the categories of military affairs, unemployment, social insurance, and civil and criminal courts, the federal government has legislative authority, but implementation is left to the cantons. In the areas of taxation, road construction, health insurance, education and training, the federal government and the cantons share power. The overall concept is that the central government handles only matters that are best handled at the federal level, and that the cantons are sovereign in all other matters. America would be well-advised to adopt this policy, the one our country was founded upon. The Swiss reached their current stable state only after the usual ethnic warfare. In a brief civil war in 1847, the German cantons defeated the French cantons that attempted secession. Since then, the only violence of note occurred after World War II when a French-speaking part of a predominately-German canton seceded by popular vote after years of firebombings and other relatively minor terrorist incidents.

It is also interesting to note that Switzerland does allow large numbers of aliens to live and work there (about 17% of the total population and not included in the above stats.) However, when economic conditions deteriorate in Switzerland, the foreigners are expelled, providing jobs for unemployed Swiss. America should institute this policy at once and ship home all 400,000 H-1B foreign workers.

Only two of Europe's heavily-multiethnic countries have achieved peaceful internal stability—Switzerland and Belgium—and both achieved that stability by granting regional autonomy to their various ethnic groups. The United States is no longer a monotribal nation because our minorities have grown too numerous, and our clumsy attempts to deal with the problem are propelling us to war. The smaller ethnic groups are now militarily strong enough to reassert their tribal identities. Ominously, there are growing indications that the whites are likewise returning to their tribal roots and rejecting a national identity as Americans. In both Switzerland and

Belgium the ethnic groups were geographically segregated. All these two fortunate nations had to do was simply draw up new laws formalizing regional autonomy, and then ethnic autonomy—the real goal—was automatically achieved. We do not enjoy such a clear pattern of geographic segregation here in America. Many areas like vast stretches of the rural Midwest are almost all white. Some, like the Mississippi Delta, are mainly black. Others, like Southern Texas, are approaching 100% Hispanic populations. However, the most common pattern is that every city and town of note has ethnically-exclusive areas and racially-mixed areas.

The stark reality is that we can probably not achieve ethnic autonomy like Switzerland or Belgium because we do not currently have sufficient geographic segregation. We may be able to achieve ethnic autonomy by allowing states to secede, or otherwise opt for increased autonomy. In this case, ethnic groups would tend to move to or from such areas as suited their advantage. Defusing our ethnic tensions by allowing states more autonomy would require a complete change in our legal system and large scale ethnic relocations. Although admittedly difficult and alien to our current notions of Americanism, secession and autonomy should be given serious consideration because otherwise such regional and ethnic autonomy will be achieved by civil war.

It is sobering to note that in ethnic patterns, America more nearly resembles the former Yugoslavia than Belgium or Switzerland. In Belgium and Switzerland, each group was confined almost exclusively to distinct areas, plus the capital city. In Yugoslavia each group was primarily concentrated in one area, but had scattered villages of its ethnics in the primary area of the other groups. Also, almost every city and town of note had areas of each ethnic group, just like America. This pattern of concentration increased demands for secession, and the isolated pockets of ethnics in the primary area of the other ethnic groups provided easy targets that fueled ethnic violence that snowballed into civil war. Like Yugoslavia, America is plagued by this highly combustible mixture of both ethnic concentration and ethnic dispersal.

When will increasingly quivering America become so unstable that it erupts in civil war? Again, there is no scientific formula, no mathematical equation, that will give us the year. Still, one can make projections. Objective analysis tends to indicate that the danger zone for secession begins when the majority ethnic group shrinks to 90%. At about 75%, where America is now, things get really serious. Red lights and sirens should be going off because America is becoming more ethnically, linguistically, and militarily unstable each day.

The likelihood of an ethnic group trying armed secession increases as their percentage of the population increases. It increases if they are concentrated in one portion of the nation. It increases if the nation has a land border with the country of origin of the ethnic group. It increases if they have a different language. It increases if they have a different physical appearance. It increases if they have a different religion. It increases if they have a markedly different culture. It increases if they have historic antagonisms.

Are we Americans witnessing an increase in our potential for civil war or not? Is our government becoming more imperial or not? Consider these monumental questions and draw your own conclusions.

The Establishment and Imperial Conversion

"American companies have either shifted output to low wage countries or come to buy parts and assembled products from countries like Japan. The U.S. is abandoning its status as an industrial power."—Akio Morita, cofounder and chairman of Sony Corp.

The establishment's ultimate goal? According to Michael Lind,[1] arguably America's leading analyst of our class structure, America will be transformed into a giant banana republic, with a super wealthy elite lording it over politically castrated masses of multiracial poor huddled in tin and plywood shacks, much like Brazil.

What does Mr. Lind think of a civil war upsetting the establishment's cunning plan?

" Although heavily outnumbered, the unified (wealthy) few rest secure in the knowledge that any insurgency will almost certainly dissipate in quarrels among the fragmented many rather than in open rebellion. During the Los Angeles riots, black, Hispanic, and white rioters turned on Korean middlemen rather than march on Beverly Hills."

Imperial Conversion

"Like all other imperial powers, we have acquired our dominion by our readiness to assist anyone, whether barbarian or Hellene, who may have invoked our aid."—Alcibiades, in a speech to the Athenians, 415 B.C.

---

1 Michael Lind, *The Next American Nation*, Free Press, 1995; *Harpers*, "To Have and To Have Not" by Michael Lind, June, 1995, p. 35.

How will the global elitists convert America from a democracy to an entirely undemocratic imperial system? Here is a list of their tools. Some have been previously mentioned, but are included here for completeness:

1: By shifting actual power from elected lawmakers to unelected judges, often appointed for life and beyond recall by American voters. By this method, any laws seriously interfering with the imperial agenda are being declared "unconstitutional." There is one other important historical point to keep in mind concerning democracy. The essence of democracy is that the majority rules, that the will of the majority can be expressed as laws that shape society. Therefore in theory, and usually in fact, democratic societies are relatively stable because most of the people are content with the way society is ordered, and can make necessary adjustments as condition change. In America, our democratic Constitution provided for elected representatives. Even though these representatives were mostly members of the oligarchy, or were subject to the bribery of the monied oligarchy, the system was still essentially democratic because the will of the oligarchy and the will of the people were relatively close. Nowadays, the American oligarchy is being subsumed into the international jet set oligarchy, and the working class is being subsumed into the labor pool of third-world peasantry.

2: By treaties that shift actual power from elected lawmakers to unelected international bodies like the United Nations and the International Monetary Fund, who are again too far away for American voters to get their hands on them. The people can elect almost anyone, but by employing the two weapons of appointed judges and unelected international bodies the globalists will retain the real power they have usurped. Only violent revolution or a sweep of both Congress and the White House by a radical third party can change this course of events.

3: By using the Federal Communications Commission to deny licenses to, and to harass anti-establishment alternative media, whether right-wing or left-wing. By allowing independent media and news outlets to be taken over and centralized by a handful of huge corporations owned exclusively by the global elitists.

4: By the establishment media amplifying some problems and ignoring others. For example, to hear the establishment media, one would think that the militias are the Ku Klux Klan in camo and are about to cover all America with a layer of corpses ten feet deep. I am not aware of one documented case of any militia member killing anyone. On the other hand, the police attribute 700 homicides a year to Los Angeles street gangs alone. Gang researcher Malcolm W. Klein attributed 2,166 homicides in 1991 to gangs.[2] Remarkably, when the Rev. Jesse Jackson and leaders of the NAACP address conventions of these mass murdering street gangs, the establishment press rolls over and wags its politically-correct tail.

5: By the unspoken agreement among the establishment elite that some persons are above both the law and media exposure. For example, President Clinton has been rumored to have fathered a son out of wedlock.[3] This young boy is reportedly living in poverty without any assistance from his alleged father. If President Clinton is this boy's father, then he should be required to fulfill his legal obligation to support his son in a manner appropriate to his financial resources. The truth or falsehood of this allegation should not be difficult to establish. The accusers have names and photographs of both the alleged mother and her boy, and the establishment media should

---

2 Malcom W. Klein, *The American Street Gang*, Oxford Univ. Press, 1995, p. 116.
3 George Cozi Jr., *Clinton Confidential*, Emery Dalton Books, 1995, pp. 178-180.

check it out. But they won't, because this Trilaterialist and champion of the establishment is above the law, like O.J. Simpson who also got "celebrity justice."

6: By fines disguised as trials. By the use of the IRS and other government bodies, the establishment can financially ruin any individual of modest means without convicting him. It doesn't matter if the charges have an ounce of truth or not. The targeted citizen can be bled of his last dollar by legal fees. In effect, the government can fine any dissident into bankruptcy at will.

7: By direct physical assault. Boot-and-shoot raids are increasingly the weapon of choice against targeted individuals as the power and arrogance of the elitists increases. Once again, it doesn't matter if the pretext for a raid has any legal substance, the medium is the message. If the targeted individual winds up on a slab, he was "resisting arrest."

8: By entrapment: This nifty trick has, since ABSCAM, been reserved for lower tier nobodys, often without any criminal record, whom the establishment occasionally deems fit to make an example of to prevent their like from getting any uppity notions inspired by the Bill of Rights.

9: By direct assassination.

10: By affirmative action that is destroying the concept of American citizenship and replacing it with a tiering arrangement suitable to the unfolding imperial system. Minorities will align with the global elitists for fear of losing their special privileges.

11: By open immigration that is creating an artificial labor surplus, driving down wages and impoverishing the white working class while it reduces their percentage of the population. The shrinking of both their absolute and relative wealth and voting power is breaking the traditional military monopoly of the white working class.

12: By gun control that will complete the stripping away of all remaining military power of the lower tiers, especially the white working class. One bumper sticker I saw

summed it up: *The Reason For The Second Amendment Is Becoming Obvious!*
13: By complicated and expensive procedures that effectively bar third party candidates from ballots, and by rigged rules that make it difficult for dissident candidates to win major party primaries. The money expended in clearing these hurdles make it difficult for dissidents to take their message to the people, and in effect amount to a tax on anti-establishment activity.

The establishment's tools are many and powerful, and many observers will conclude that conversion to an imperial system is assured. They may be right, but historical analysis suggests that the juggling of these various blocks and masses of poor people is simply too complex. There is too much that can go wrong. Therefore, the cataclysm of Civil War II is more likely than a completed imperial conversion.

Welcome to Brazil

"The worst of the settlements provide a harrowing glimpse of life on the ragged edges of subsistence, with conditions that are being described as a growing slice of the third world within the United States."—Peter Applebome speaking on "colonia" slums that have sprouted on our side of the Mexican/US border—*New York Times* Mar. 3, 1988

Are the rich getting richer and the workers getting poorer? More broadly, are the elite actually making any progress in their overall plan to transform America into a third-world country? There is no mathematical equation or scientific formula that will give us an exact answer. However, let's take what projections we have and see when America will join the ranks of the third world.

Projections 1 and 2: Demographics

1: Year America has a nonwhite majority: 2050
2: Year Border states have a Hispanic majority: 2031

Projection number one is the approximate date America will no longer have a white majority—2050, and projection two is the year the border states will have a Hispanic majority. Other factors also serve to identify third-world countries, and low wages is a standout.

Projection 3: The Shrinking hourly wage

For projection number three, we shall define our arrival at third-world status when the average hourly wage sinks to the level of our current federal minimum wage of $4.25 an hour. We shall base this projection on the year 1973, the year America began to feel the effects of the deliberate transformation to a third-world, undemocratic, racist imperial system. According to the U.S. Bureau of Labor Statistics, the average hourly wage in constant 1982 (adjusted for inflation) dollars for private industry was $8.55 in 1973 and $7.39 in 1993.[4] That's a 14% drop in 20 years. That's a lot.

The minimum federal wage of $4.25 is 39% of $10.83 1993 wage. When will the average wage be 38% of our current wage if present trends continue? In the year 2071, the average hourly wage will be $2.83 in 1982 dollars, or 38% of our current hourly wage of $7.40 in 1982 dollars. If present trends continue, in 2078 the average wage will be the minimum wage. Granted, 2078 is a long way off (though such trends do tend to accelerate). Still, if you are the parent of a newly-born child, it means that your child will live to see an America where the average worker is a minimum wage worker. How large do you suppose your child's social security check will be when the average worker is getting minimum wage? To put a human face on this trend of dropping wages, it means that children born at the time of the publishing of this book will die prematurely because they will be

---

4 US Dept. of Labor Bureau of Labor Statistics, Sept. 1994, *Bulletin 2445*, p. 4.

living in a third-world country unable to feed them when they are old and no longer able to work. In the future, the American dream will be a garbage dump with only a few other people to fight for the scraps.

The epithet of American children born from now on will be: *Born in America, Starved in Brazil.* According to the American Institute for the Advancement of Science, "Exhausted land, scarce water, and a doubling in population will combine to radically change the American diet by 2050, with less meat and dairy products, more grains and beans, and a sparser variety of vegetables . . ."[5] Dr. David Pimentel of Cornell University has projected that America will cease to be a food exporter by 2025 if present trends continue.

As this book goes to press, the steady erosion of wages is starting to receive much attention in the establishment press, and is becoming a political issue. Do not be misled by those who claim that workers are actually better off than they were in the early 1970's. Statistics such as rising median family income will be cited by some to back up their false claims that Americans are better off than ever. For example, median family incomes have been rising because more and more American wives have been forced to start working because their husbands' wages have been falling. The most honest measure of the state of the American worker is the one cited here—the average hourly wage adjusted for inflation. It's a measure of what the typical American worker can actually get in the labor market, what he is actually worth in real terms.

P3: Average hourly wage hits minimum wage level: 2071

---

5 *The New York Times*, Feb. 18, 1995, p. 8.

Projection 4: Foreigners Hold Most Federal Debt

Another typical statistic of third-world countries is their governments' indebtedness to foreigners. The elites of third-world countries loot their own powerless poor until they have so little left it's hardy worth stealing. At that point they turn to the international money markets. What does the US economic establishment think of foreign dominance of our country? Consider this passage from a recent *Wall Street Journal* editorial titled "The Next Fifty Years":[6]

"We'll settle happily for a whole world growing richer under Asia's economic lead, but the challenge facing the region isn't asserting leadership in the face of a jealous and declining West. It's the management of Asia's internal rivalries . . . ."

What they failed to mention is that the working people of America aren't growing richer. In fact, they've been sinking since the seventies. In America the rich really are getting richer and the workers poorer exactly as blueprinted. Why bother to risk investing in new factories that might fail when they can get a guaranteed return on US government bonds? That foreigners are also buying up that debt and taking over our country and turning it into a huge Tijuana doesn't bother them at all. When foreigners hold more federal debt than American citizens, it will be another plain sign that America is just another third-world country. How far away is that? In 1969, only 5% of our federal debt was held by foreigners. In 1990, that figure had grown to 17%.[7] At this rate, most federal debt will be held by foreigners by the year 2048. Since trends like this tend to accelerate as economic conditions worsen,

6 The Wall Street Journal, "The Next Fifty Years", August 14, 1995, p. 16.
7 Don Barlett and James Steele, *America, What Went Wrong?*, Andrews and McMell Books, 1992, p. 50.

the date most US debt is held by foreigners may come much sooner than 2048.

P4: Most federal debt is held by foreigners: 2048

Projection 5: 20 Million in Third-World Slums

Third-world slums began appearing in our southwest all along our border with Mexico in the 1980s, and they are steadily expanding just like cancers. They're called "Colonias," which is Spanish for new neighborhoods or colonies. In fact, these colonias are Mexican colonies on our soil—typical Mexican slums inhabited partially, if not mainly, by illegal Mexican aliens. That's how *The New York Times* described these slums ". . . colonies of Mexico, ringers for settlements just south of the border."[8]

These colonias are created by greedy landowners who divide up their land into tiny lots, and then sell or rent them to desperately poor Hispanics in need of housing. The developers of these slums don't develop them at all. They build no houses, put in no sewers, pave no streets, lay no water pipes, put up no power lines, arrange for no garbage pickup—nothing. They just carve up their land into tiny parcels and collect the money. The desperately poor Hispanics, many of them illegal aliens, then build whatever shacks on these lots that their humble means allow.

The New York Times described these colonias as ". . . rusted trailers and shacks nailed together from tar paper and packing pallets." "Without indoor toilets." With mounds of uncollected trash that "attract large rats." Commenting on the lack of sewers and water hookups, the *Times* said, "The lack

---

8 *The New York Times*, "Along US Border, a Third World is Reborn", March 3, 1988, p. 1; *The New York Times*, "At Texas Border, Hopes for Sewers and Water", Jan. 3, 1989, p. 12; *The New York Times*, "The Cholera Watch", March 22, 1992, Sect. C, p. 32; *The New York Times*, April 2, 1995, Business Sect., p. 1.

of sanitation has polluted the water underground to the point that many residents are literally drinking their own wastes." The colonias have third-world levels of hepatitis, dysentery, diarrhea, skin rashes, and tuberculosis; and are "ground zero" for a possible cholera epidemic. The residents of these colonias typically store their drinking water in 55 gallon industrial drums which are, according to the El Paso Health Director Dr. Lawrence Nickery, "contaminated with fecal bacteria and every carcinogen on the list."

Here are some of the words the *Times* used in their articles about these colonias: "chaotic, contaminated, crisis, despair, disenfranchised, explosive, fecal, filth, glaring, illegal, inadequate, jumbled, misery, neglect, pain, polluted, poor, poverty, powder keg, problems, putrid, ramshackle, shanties, shocking, sick, slum, stench, struggle, suffering, tragic, unsanitary, wrenching." Get the picture?

Since their appearance in Texas about ten years ago, these Mexican slums on American soil have spread all along the border from Brownsville, Texas to San Diego, California. According to the Times, the 1988 total population of the border colonias was 185,000—the 1995 total was 500,000.[9] If the colonias keep growing at this rate, their combined total population will equal the current population of Mexico City—about 20 million—in the year 2021.

Think about it. It will be as if the entire 20 million inhabitants of Mexico City packed, crossed the Rio Grande and squatted on American soil. To begin with, these third-world slums represent a serious and growing health hazard. Also, they are depressing the wage levels, driving whites, especially working-class whites, out of the border area. I personally know one young white man who was forced to abandon Texas for this very reason. America now has a

---

9 Television program *Sixty Minutes*, October 8, 1995.

growing population of internal white refugees who are fleeing these growing stains of the third-world on American soil.[10]

P5: USA Third-World slums reach 20 million—2021

How dangerous are these third-world colonia slums? Eventually, all of southern California will be a vast third-world colonia slum, and dead center of the 100 mile by 100 mile L.A. colonia will be the epicenter and ground zero of Civil War II.

Based on the mutual reinforcement and therefore certain acceleration of the trends listed above, I expect Civil War II will shift into its all-out, continuous military phase sooner than the above figures indicate. Not to be accused of stinginess, I'll even give the exact time and place:

The Year: 2020
The Date: The Fifth of May
The Time: About Midnight
The State: California
The City: Los Angeles
The Place: Ruben Salazar Park

What About Reform ?

"There are a thousand hacking at the branches of evil to one who is striking at its root."—Henry David Thoreau

———   ———

10 I wonder if the Maequiladora factories were built remotely situated hard up against our border to destabilize our border area and detach it from America. By the device of the Maequiladora factories, the Mexican side of the border was flooded with Mexicans to make the American side dependent on Mexico economically, to facilitate massive illegal immigration when slumps occurred in Maequiladora employment, and to eventually drive out of the border zone every last Anglo due to the escalating crime on the American side perpetrated by impoverished Mexicans. It's working.

There are, in theory, several scenarios for the future of America. They are, in order of possibility of occurrence:

(1) A second Civil War, and the subsequent partitioning of America into several new ethnically-based nations.

(2) Completed imperial conversion, and the transformation of America into an undemocratic, multiethnic, poverty-stricken, third-world empire.

(3) The peaceful breakup of America into three or more ethnically-based nations.

(4) America remaining intact by the will of the people, a possibility only if two conditions are met: (A) Reforms are instituted to turn over political power to the people and to permanently stop the massive, institutionalized corruption that now permeates every phase of our government. (B) Massive and voluntary assimilation of various tribal groups.

Unfortunately, the order of desirability of these scenarios is exactly the opposite of their likelihood of occurrence. To be technically correct, the prospect of a second civil war would be preferable to completed imperial conversion if there were some guarantee that the postwar states would be democratic, and the war itself would not be overly destructive. I do not believe that the Hispanic and black nations rising out of the ashes of postwar America will be democratic in any meaningful sense or as prosperous as current-day America. In the long run, I think the new white America will be more democratic and a more pleasant and prosperous place to live than current-day America, but a second civil war is still a hefty butcher's bill to pay for the benefit of future white Americans.

To point out the near impossibility of the the fourth (and most desirable) scenario, one only has to consider the reforms necessary to bring it about. These reforms would necessarily be so extensive that they would require many amendments to our Constitution. These reforms will not be put in place because they would require that the international oligarchy relinquish its power and it is not about to do that peacefully.

Waco, Ruby Ridge and Oklahoma City

"Laws are like cobwebs, for any trifling or powerless thing falls into them, they hold it fast; but if a thing of any size falls into them, it breaks the mesh and escapes."—Anacharsis

These tragedies can not be understood unless examined from the proper perspective, the perspective of Civil War II. Because we're abandoning our common identity as Americans, people are turning to alternate sources of psychological fulfillment and the increasingly necessary military protection that these groups are extending. The Waco cult was partly a manifestation of this trend, and partly the creation of David Koresh. I would be appalled if someone I cared for announced that they were thinking of joining the Branch Davidians, and I would try anything short of violence to stop them from doing so.

I believe David Koresh was a criminal psychopath, but I also believe everyone is entitled to respectful and courteous treatment, and due process. *After all, I might be wrong*, and that's exactly why we have due process, so that individuals like Koresh may defend themselves. Everyone is entitled to due process and equal protection of the law; that's what it means to be a civilized society. Unfortunately, this is not the view of the Washington establishment.

The federal government was acting partly like a democratic government in a sincere attempt to protect the children of the Waco cult from alleged abuse and to seize alleged illegal guns. However, the federal government was also acting like an imperial government as evidenced by its Vietnam-style search and destroy assault against the Waco compound. The ongoing transformation of the federal government from a law respecting democratic system into a law-violating imperial system was reflected in the hybrid conduct of the federal police at Waco.

The cultists were genuinely terrified by the ATF, as witnessed by their 911 call to the local police. Their 911 call also testified as to their willingness to submit to the law. But their plea for the protection of the law went unanswered, and they rightfully defended themselves rather than submit to the usual ATF boot-and-shoot perversion of justice.

Even if the cultists fired first, they were right to do so because no truly free persons should ever have to put up with a search and destroy assault unless they have been first asked to surrender after a polite knock on the door by someone who looks like a civilized law enforcement officer. Any honest person will admit that the police would never mount one of these Robo Cop assaults on Ted Kennedy's home if identical accusations were made against him. The cultists were not escaped convicts on the run. They were merely accused of violating some laws, and they should have been treated with respect and presumption of innocence, and not punished until convicted by a court of law.

The police defend these Vietnam-style raid tactics, saying that a massive assault of manpower and firepower intimidates their objects, who then peacefully surrender, thus saving both their lives and the lives of the police. As for the allegation that police lives are saved by these boot and shoot tactics, it didn't save any police lives at Waco. And in any case, the duty of the police is not to look first after their own lives, but to protect the lives, property and rights of citizens even to the point of risking their own lives. That's what it means to be a professional law enforcement officer of a civilized nation.

Any policeman who thinks safeguarding his own life is a justification for these gestapo tactics is not fit to be a policeman, plain and simple. And if the police were really concerned with safeguarding innocent lives, they would never assault with bullet spraying automatic weapons where children are present as at Waco. The ATF and FBI are merely rationalizing tactics forced upon them by their ongoing conversion into military arms of the emerging multiethnic American Empire. Sadly, most FBI and ATF agents aren't aware of the true nature of the situation and genuinely think themselves blameless.

Recall that in empires, laws are a facade and power is the only thing that really counts. Any imperial government that isn't strong enough to shove various groups into their assigned stations will soon find all those it had previously bullied and bluffed into submission standing up to it. Therefore, the federal government had no choice but to demonstrate it was still the biggest, baddest bully on the block. Imperial governments can not seriously appeal to the citizens to obey the law because imperial governments themselves are the greatest violators of the law. So the stage was set for the tragedy.

The government laid siege to the cultists, cut off their food and electricity, blared horrible noises at them, restricted their access to the media, broadcast all manner of unproven accusations against them, shot stun grenades at them, and overflew the compound with helicopters at all hours. All these willful torments were cynical demonstrations of naked power by a bruised and insecure bully determined to publicly flex his muscles. Then came the final assault—tanks knocking down walls, CS gas that induces vomiting and can kill a child.

The popular perception of CS gas is that it's some sort of mild, tear inducing irritant that makes your eyes water till you cry. That's not the case. I was exposed to CS gas in the army, and it's like trying to breath flaming gasoline. You absolutely think you're going to die, and you will in fact die if the concentration is too high. If you lock a man in a room the size of a bathroom, toss in a CS grenade, then seal the room, that man will die within 15 minutes.

Here's what *The New Yorker* reported about the gas attack on the Waco compound in their May 15, 1995 issue:[1]

"The F.B.I. pumped tear gas into the compound periodically during the first hours of the assault until the supply of gas was exhausted. Then agents sent to Houston for more, and exhausted that supply, too."

Even *The New Yorker* was apparently put off by the brutality of the gas attack, even thought they didn't say so explicitly. As for the fire, the government knew there were open flames and therefore they knew there was a chance of fire when they sent their tanks to knock down the walls, supposing, of course, that the children inside hadn't been crushed to death when the tanks knocked down the walls in the first place. The government knowingly introduced, or their callous indifference caused to be introduced, three potentially fatal elements during the final assault—tanks, fire and gas—and the results were indeed fatal.

In summary, the government's initial search and destroy raid was a bullyboy operation and the bullyboy got whipped by the perceived nobodys he thought he could pick on without fear of being hit back. Consider a certain New England senator, a certain black Islamic cult or a certain pedophile entertainer. All have had legal difficulties involving firearms, sex, sex with children, and even allegations of murder, but no tank assaults were mounted against them. They're members of higher tiers in the American Empire based on their wealth or ethnic group or membership in the establishment, as opposed to the mainly white and relatively poor Waco cultists.

The government responded to criticism with public relations double-talk. They gave the FBI agent in charge a mild rebuke, then did an about-face and said he'd be promoted. The promotion was the real signal, the signal that stormtrooper tactics are the sure road to promotion for ambitious young imperial stormtroopers, as long, of course, as they're

1 *The New Yorker, Magazine*, "The Children of Waco", May 15, 1995, p. 45.

only used against those in the empire's lower tiers—not the previously mentioned senator, cult leader or entertainer, or their similarly privileged equivalents.

The Assassinations at Ruby Ridge

Randy Weaver was a white separatist. Our Bill of Rights absolutely protects the right of Mr. Weaver to hold this and any other opinion, but the Constitution means nothing to the imperial stormtroopers. Randy Weaver had broken no laws, not a single law, not one, period. Mr. Weaver was targeted for a takeout solely because of his political views, plain and simple. The federal agents paid one of their agent provocateurs to entrap Mr. Weaver into violating a minor firearms law. The agent provocateur paid the hard-up Mr. Weaver to saw the barrel of a legal shotgun down to an illegal length. The feds entrapped Mr. Weaver to recruit him as an agent provocateur who would entrap other white separatists and inform on them.

Mr. Weaver manfully refused, which is also his absolute right. But rights mean nothing to the arrogant FBI and ATF. Recall that in undemocratic societies the police freely combine the role of police and judge, and summarily punish all who dare defy them. If you don't like it, that's tough, and be advised you better get used to the fact because it's here to stay.

Mr. Weaver was arrested and given a date to appear before a court. Mr. Weaver rightfully and manfully refused to meekly play this game with the court. To those who object to my defense of Mr. Weaver's refusal to appear in court I have this to say: Any truly honest person will admit that Ted Kennedy would never be likewise entrapped by federal agents. *Any law that is not equally applied to all is not a law but a truncheon used to beat those who legally hold opinions opposed to the establishment*—opinions protected by our Bill of Rights.[2]

The establishment then sent their federal thugs to kidnap Mr. Weaver, who manfully and rightfully defended his life and liberty. The federal agents mounted one of their usual search and destroy sieges complete with the usual snipers, armored vehicles, and helicopters. FBI snipers gunned down Mr. Weaver's dog, and fatally shot Mr. Weaver's son in the back. A federal agent was also shot dead, allegedly by a friend of Mr. Weaver's. A federal sniper then shot Mr. Weaver's wife dead while she was holding her infant in her arms.

To those who say it can't happen here, let them go to Ruby Ridge.

Mr. Weaver then surrendered. He was acquitted of murder and other charges, and convicted only of failing to appear for his original trial on the firearms charge. He should have been acquitted of all charges, and the federal assassins put on trial for murder. As this book is written, investigations are starting to reveal that federal agents destroyed documents that reveal their guilt. If the federal agents escape with a slap, it will not be forgotten. They are not the only ones with power.

It is never a legitimate function of the police of a free society to monitor the political opinions of anyone—never, not under any circumstances, without exception. Such police monitoring can never be legitimate because all political views are legal in a free society—all of them, absolutely, without exception. The police should concern themselves exclusively with actual violations of laws. When the police monitor and/or entrap persons based on their political opinions, they are siding with one political faction against another, and they thus slip into an abyss of their own excavation and become the secret police of a totalitarian system. Entrapment will be an increasingly-employed weapon in the arsenal of the global

---

2 Because of numerous and conflicting accounts of the Ruby Ridge affair, I am unable to determine if Mr. Weaver intentionally refused to show up for his court date, or if he did not appear due to a mix-up in the court documents. I have assumed he knowingly refused to appear in order to to make it clear that he was right to do so in that case.

imperialists, but of course only against non-establishment targets. Mr. Weaver was entrapped with cash. Marion Barry, the Mayor Washington D.C., was entrapped with drugs and a woman. Guess, just for fun, how many of our congressmen would snap at the tantalizing bait of money, whores, and the intoxicant of their choice.[3] The federal police are no longer servants of the people, but private security thugs in the employ of the global, imperialist establishment. If they wish rational people to believe otherwise, then they must regularly entrap Congressmen, an obviously easy task given the thievery that Washington vibrates to.

The Oklahoma City Bombing

The Oklahoma City bombing was mass murder and terrorism. I hope that those responsible are apprehended, tried and executed. Also, I don't think for a second that federal agents were responsible.[4] We must analyze the Oklahoma City bombing from the Civil War II perspective.

Recall that in imperial systems, the law is a facade and power is the only thing that really counts. Bombs are literally power, and the bombers were playing by the rules the feds themselves laid down at Waco and Ruby Ridge: The law doesn't count, only power really counts, so screw the law and show everybody that you've got the power.

---

3 One does wonder just what Marion Barry did that the establishment baited its trap for him.

4 Although the feds have truck-bombed women and children when it served their purposes in the past. In the May 1995 issue of *The Nation* magazine, Alexander Cockburn recounted how CIA agents set off a truck bomb that killed 80 and wounded 256 people, many of them women and children, on March 8, 1985 in a suburb of Beirut, Lebanon. The CIA wanted to take out some radical Moslem holy man, Mohammed something or other, and they did not shrink from killing the women and children they knew full well would be present in the vicinity of his suburban headquarters. They missed the Moslem cleric, by the way.

Federal agents bashing down the doors of militiamen and others will not stop the terrorism because the militiamen and such are not the root cause of the terrorism. Additionally, the FBI and ATF, however much their repulsive and illegal tactics contribute to the escalating terrorism, are not its ultimate cause either. The underlying cause is the ongoing transformation of America into an undemocratic, multiethnic empire.

The Waco search and destroy, the Ruby Ridge assassinations, and the Oklahoma City bombing are the initial skirmishes in the war that must be fought, and is being fought, as part of the Imperial Conversion process. Therefore, things will not get better. They will get increasingly worse until the transformation is completed or the empire breaks up via civil war into separate, ethnically-based nations. Technically speaking, America is now going through the second of four phases of Civil War II, a transitional phase of intermittent terrorism by both the federal government and the resisters that will grow into a guerrilla warfare stage, and eventually culminate in the continuous, all-out military phase of Civil War II.

The establishment simply has no option. They absolutely have to publicly and repeatedly violate the Bill of Rights, all while they publicly deny that they are doing so. The Bill of Rights must be gutted and remade into a facade of euphemisms, and the more obvious the facade the better.

This facade will serve as a sort of pagan idol to test people. Those who bow down signal their submission; those who do not will soon find themselves objects of the establishment's attention. Either way, the idol of a facade serves it sole purpose, to let the establishment know who submits and who does not. That's why the facade must be completely obvious, because only then can it serve as a test of those who submit and those who do not. To be technically accurate, some of those who bow down won't understand that they are submitting. That is to say, they have internalized the racist euphemisms of the new order to such a degree that they are indistinguishable from Pavlovian dogs who salivate on command. They have lost the ability to reason, and react only on a stimulus response basis.

The communists had a clever tag for such people that advanced their cause—useful idiots. There's a big downside to being a useful idiot. When they outlive their usefulness to the establishment, then they will be use*less* idiots. They will be thrown overboard to appease some other tier of the empire that needs appeasing, just as the Democrat Party discarded the white working class to get the vote of the blacks who are block voters.

Also, Waco and Ruby Ridge served other purposes. First, the establishment must harden into shape a brutal gang of imperial stormtroopers something like the USSR's KGB to make sure the lower-tier peasants stay in their assigned place. All this kicking in of doors is a sort of on the job training to purge those not up to standards, that is to say those with some remaining hint of decency and therefore infinitely unworthy to stand tall in the ranks of the Imperial Police. Secondly, operations like Waco and Ruby Ridge provoke reactions from Resisters, and the Oklahoma City bombing was almost certainly such a reaction. These reactions are a windfall for the establishment, as they can be used as an excuse for even more assaults on the Bill of Rights.

The President should have demanded the resignation of Attorney General Janet Reno, who clearly has haunted house music playing in her head, and the principal FBI strategist behind Waco and Ruby Ridge, a Mr. Potts. But he didn't, and America edged that much closer to Civil War II.

The Resisters (I shall proʊume) replied in the only language the establishment understands in order that justice be done for the FBI and ATF victims, and innocent people died. The Oklahoma City bombing put Waco and Ruby Ridge back in the news. Since Oklahoma City, Potts got a slap; he was demoted from the number two man at the FBI to head a training facility. Pott's transfer to a training facility was meant to be perceived as punishment, and hopefully the resisters are satisfied, but I doubt it.

All these tragedies could have been avoided if the establishment had substituted obedience to the law for public demonstrations of brute power, but that's incompatible with our unfolding imperial system. From the establishment's point of view, these three operations advanced their agenda, and were therefore successful, as evidenced by the initial promotion of the commander at Waco. Nothing succeeds like success, so expect more such mileposts as we march through Waco, Ruby Ridge, Oklahoma City, and future similar take-outs on our way to Civil War II.

Prepare Yourself

"Fiddle-dee-dee. War, war, war. This war talk's spoiling all the fun at every party this spring. I get so bored I could scream. Besides, there isn't going to be any war!"—Scarlett O'Hara in *Gone With the Wind*

In Civil War II your survivability factor will be determined much as the cost of real estate—Location! Location! Location! The most probable outcome of Civil War II is the partition of current America into several new ethnically-based nations. When the war breaks out and the country breaks down, you want to be already living safe and sound in the new nation carved out by your tribe, so move there as soon as your circumstances allow.

But don't drop everything and head for Idaho today; there is no need for rash action. You still have some years in which to arrange your affairs to your advantage. And if you play your cards right, you will minimize the impact of the war on yourself and your family. It's aces and eights for America, but it doesn't have to be that way for you.

First, realize that areas with mixed tribal populations will experience the most fighting, employment of heavy weapons, and general devastation of life and infrastructure. Regardless of which side wins, these areas will look like the the Yugoslavia we've all seen on TV. If you currently live in such an area you must move out. Likewise, you must sell all non-movable assets in such areas or risk losing them, either by destruction or confiscation by the new government, a certainty if the new government is not of your tribe.

Also be advised that the economic impact of Civil War II will be felt in these mixed areas long before the outbreak of all-out war. The eye of the Civil War II hurricane turns hundreds of miles offshore, but its outermost winds are already lifting the hair of those on the beach. Anglos in the southwest are abandoning the Reconquista lands, seeking refuge in the Pacific Northwest and Rocky Mountain states. The establishment press has mocked this historic movement, calling it "Valhallaism," after the home of the Nordic gods. Let them laugh. In time they will Valhalla out themselves. Other anglos, mostly affluent professionals, are stockading themselves in walled and guarded suburbs all over the southwest. This neo-medieval strategy is another pathetic and fatal exercise in self-deception.

As imperial America spirals downward, real estate prices in the Reconquista lands will slide, mirrored by an increase in the value of land in the Valhalla regions. The longer you stay, the greater risk you expose yourself to. You must move to that portion of current America which will be within the boundaries of the new nation of your tribe. But you must also consider which exact area within the new nation is optimum for survival. Certain areas should be avoided.

First, avoid the area bordering the other new nations. The border zone will be one of military activity, in some cases quite intense. By all means stay a minimum of 30 miles from the border, the approximate range of heavy artillery. Also, large portions of border areas may be handed over to the other new nations as part of final peace negotiations, as was the case in the war in the former Yugoslavia. As a rule of thumb, the farther into the interior of the new nation, the better.

Second, avoid areas of the new nation that are dependent on water or electricity or gas pipelines which originate in or pass through the other new (and hostile) nations. These inputs will cut off during the war, and perhaps even permanently cut off after active military hostilities cease.

Third, avoid areas near military bases. There will be varying degrees of fighting around these bases until the issue of management is settled, and there will be collateral damage to surrounding areas. As a rule of thumb, stay the distance of light weapons from these bases, say a minimum of five miles. Fourth, within the new nation avoid areas near enclaves of outsiders, persons not of your tribe. As with military bases, these areas will experience fighting to one degree or another. For example, if you are thinking about moving to the state of Washington, which will certainly be within the new white nation, avoid suburbs of Seattle that are adjacent to nonwhite suburbs, or which will likely be adjacent to nonwhite suburbs as demographic patterns change. Again, a good rule of thumb is a minimum of five miles from such areas. Better yet, avoid all large cities with sizable enclaves of minorities, which realistically means all large cities.

These are the four primary considerations that will determine the survival of people and infrastructure during the war. If you follow these straightforward rules your local area will be free from almost all military activity, and all the amenities of life such as electricity and running water will function with only minimum interruption. Still, there are other important considerations that should cause you to avoid areas that satisfy all the above limiting parameters.

Consider how prosperous the area will be during and after the war. Some areas are dependent on economic activities and patterns that will be negatively impacted or disappear entirely. Consider, for example, Hawaii. Hawaii will likely be an area of intense fighting due to its ethnic mix, population density and abundance of military bases. However, let us assume for illustration that these problems did not exist. Hawaii would still be a terrible place to be caught because it is dependent on the tourist trade, which will largely disappear during the war, and worse yet Hawaii is entirely dependent on imported food. With the tourist trade shut down and the importation of food disrupted by the fighting on the continent, Hawaii will be a scenic death trap for those stranded there. The same rule generally applies to Las Vegas, but at least it will be easier to evacuate. In this matter I can chiefly give guidelines only at the conceptual level. You yourself will have to analyze any given local area. Ask yourself how its economic patterns will be impacted by the war. The last thing you want is to be residing in an area of desperate, hungry and armed people. One rule of thumb worth considering is choosing the smallest town possible given your circumstances. In Civil War II as in all wars, cities will tend to attract refugees in direct proportion to their size, and lawlessness always follows such unfortunate people.

Another possibility worthy of at least passing consideration is living in a remote area, an area where hunting and fishing are a real option for supplying significant portions of your food, and where personal safety is obviously maximized. Personally, I don't think this feature should be given much consideration in choosing a living site. First, I think storing food is more practical, and hunting requires more skill than you may be able to acquire prior to starving to death. Also, I think that smaller towns will be almost perfectly safe, and therefore there will be no real need for the absolute safety of having no neighbors. Also consider an area that is not excessively frigid in winter. Fuel is always dear in war, and often unavailable at any price. Avoid areas in which you could actually freeze to death in winter without fuel. Likewise, try to select an site with a short commute to work, again because fuel will be at a premium.

And what should you do after the move? Keep in mind that these monotribal regions are only relatively safe, not absolutely safe. While these regions will be outside the zone of most large scale military actions, no region of America will be entirely spared the consequences of the economic and social chaos of Civil War II. These consequences, as mentioned earlier, could range up to bandenkreig and mass starvation, all depending on the scope and duration of the war, neither of which can be calculated at this time. Therefore, even if you live in an essentially nonmilitary zone, you should take some minimum precautions.

First, you should stockpile food, at least enough to sustain yourself and your family for one year. And don't tell anyone about it, or your hoarded food will likely cost you your life.

Technical specifics for food stockpiling can be gotten from various survivalist books. The individuals who concern themselves with such matters know vastly more about it than I do. In this area, I pretend no expertise and dispense none.

Second, get a gun. Again, don't tell anyone. Unregistered weapons are better, as the attitude of the government (and nongovernmental armed bands!) in all areas will likely be subject to extreme oscillation. For most people, the gun selected should be a semiautomatic rifle that fires a standard military cartridge, standard cartridges being more readily available during war than nonstandard ones. Certainly you should stockpile ammunition; about 5,000 rounds should be sufficient. By all means get a good quality telescopic sight for your rifle, a dozen large capacity magazines, and all necessary cleaning gear.

One excellent choice is the Mini-14 5.56 caliber rifle. It fires the standard military cartridge, and this versatile weapon has a wide selection of accessories available. My chief problem with the Mini 14's 5.56 round is that it will not be the optimum round for the military environment of Civil War II. To understand why, we shall have to take a brief sidetrip and recall why it (and similar light rounds) became the standard military cartridges.

After World War II, the military of the Western nations came to broadly similar conclusions: That most infantry fighting (and therefore rifle kills) occurred at relatively close range, usually 100 meters or less, and that most hits resulted from random shots fired in the general direction of the enemy rather than aimed shots at observed enemy soldiers. (They are a lot harder to see than in the movies, they camouflage themselves and take cover.)

Therefore, the realistic way to increase hits was to increase the number of shots fired. Since a soldier can carry only so much weight, the generals deduced that the only way to increase the number of shots fired was to decrease the weight of the rounds, thereby allowing an increase in the total number of rounds carried and fired. And since the range at which most infantry fighting occurred was 100 yards or less, the shorter combat effective range of these lighter rounds would seldom be a drawback. To paraphrase a certain lite beer commercial—More killing, less weight! My own military experience largely verifies the conclusion of the generals, but more about that in a moment. Other factors also increased the universal shift to lighter caliber assault rifles: The reduced chamber pressures made the lighter rifles cheaper to produce, and the lighter ammo promised to reduce resupply difficulties, always an important factor in wartime. Increases in the use of cramped vehicles and helicopters to transport troops also encouraged the shift to shorter, lighter rifles. The promise of arms sales in non-Western nations where the soldiers are often of less stature and therefore more suited to lighter arms was also a factor. And some generals reckoned that the emphasis on the "spray and pray" philosophy inherent in the lighter weapons would allow less marksmanship training for recruits, thus allowing for greater training facility "throughput" in times of massive wars. My point in mentioning these other factors is that a little thought reveals that they should not be factors in your selection of a rifle.

On the whole, I agree with the spray-and-pray reason for the shift to the lighter caliber assault rifles, but I also maintain that the military pendulum is swinging back to the heaver caliber cartridges with their longer range and greater penetrating power. Why? For one thing bullet resistant vests are now standard issue for grunts, and for good reason—they're getting better all the time as exotic new materials for them are being developed. I think the 7.62 standard NATO round (not the short Russian AK47 version) should now be the standard size round considering the impact these vests are having on infantry fighting. By the way, be sure to get a vest yourself. Even if you don't take part in the fighting, it may save you from being a sniper's snack when you're making a run for whatever. There is no hurry to obtain a vest because they are not currently subject to legal bans, and the longer you wait the better the vests available.

Another big reason the big calibers are making a come-back is the increasing role that telescopic sights are having in infantry combat. The 7.62 NATO round can kill at greater distances than the lighter 5.56, but using iron sights the average grunt can't hit the opera fat lady at 200 meters, so why bother with the heavier cartridges? With telescopic sights now common, the longer range of the heavier cartridges can be taken advantage of.

Another reason I recommend the heavier cartridges is that they are more suited to the type of fighting peculiar to Yugoslav-style civil wars, which will also be the most common mode of infantry fighting here, at least in the early stages. Most of the fighters, at least in the early stages, will be civilians, and therefore most of the fighting will take place where the fighters live—in the cities and suburbs, as opposed to the continuous front fighting of World War II which meant that most fighting was rural. In urban fighting there are often unobstructed views for hundreds of meters, or the opportunity for such views in the three dimensional environment provided by buildings. Also, these urban areas tend to have a higher ratio of fighters to space because of the importance of the retaining the city, and again because the fighters live there. In short, the concrete urban jungle is target-rich and predator-friendly even at extreme distances, and such an environment is scope country, so bring yours . . . and keep concealed.

Finally, I expect the greater part of Civil War II fighting to be static, not assault-oriented as in conventional warfare. In conventional warfare infantry must ultimately stand and close with opposing infantry, thus the "assault" designation of their standard rifle. In such circumstances a garden hose-type weapon is obviously the optimum one for both team victory and personal survival. In Civil War II, as in Yugoslavia, much of the fighting will consist of local forces securing their local area, particularly after the initial and chaotic fighting. The static nature inherent in this situation calls for longer range weapons, and places no great bonus on automatic fire or lightness of weight, at least not in individual weapons.

I recommend caching your firearm, ammunition and all accessories at some location that has no connection to you in the event that your cache is found. Burial is one option, and suitable containers and methods for caching by burial can be had from various survivalist suppliers. Even if you cache your firearm at some remote location I again recommend that you break it down and cache it in several locations so that if one portion is found it can not be fired. Also, I recommend that you cache only non-registered firearms so that they can not be traced to you if found. There is no one solution to the many problems that attend storage of firearms; it is your responsibility to weigh all the factors and determine which options suits your mix of circumstances.

I strongly recommend against keeping a firearm in the home. Each year, many children kill themselves playing with home-kept firearms, and such a tragedy can happen even though you take the strictest precautions such as locking your gun in a cabinet. Furthermore, even experienced and professional gun handlers such as policemen and soldiers frequently shoot themselves while handling their firearms. I've almost been shot by accidentally discharged firearms more times than I can recall at one sitting. And with only one exception it was by someone familiar with firearms, someone who had been trained in their handling and knew better. They simply screwed up, just as you will too if you handle firearms long enough. Firearms are inherently dangerous, plain and simple, even in the hands of an expert.

The truth is that the more you handle a firearm, the more likely you are to accidentally kill yourself or someone else, so never handle a firearm unless it is a necessity. Firing a rifle is fun, I'll admit, but I would never consider firing a rifle solely for fun just as I would never go to the dentist for fun. The only circumstances under which I will handle a firearm is to kill someone or to practice killing someone. Period! You would be well advised to adopt the same attitude and never touch a firearm without a businesslike cause. I also adamantly recommend against pistols. First, they are essentially useless for real combat, and are therefore a waste of money better spent elsewhere. Also, they are by far the most inherently dangerous firearm. When you handle them your trigger finger almost automatically comes in contract with the trigger, and Murphy's Law comes into play.

Personally, if my firearm were not traceable to me, I would cache it away from my home, and retrieve it once a year for maintenance and perhaps a little target practice. If circumstances forced me to keep my rifle at home I would take some basic precautions. I would field strip it and cache it in several different places so that it could not be fired without being re-assembled, and the several cache places would be both hidden and locked. Hidden to prevents its removal by government agents and other thieves, and locked to prevent children and childish adults from handling the firearm. The ammunition would likewise be kept hidden and locked.

If you are a young person you should consider the impact of Civil War II on your choice of occupations. The war years and the immediate postwar years will involve a different sort of economy than the current one. First, consider that many current occupations exist only in a rather artificial way, sustained by a relatively affluent and government-directed economy. To give but one example there are people who dig up and study dinosaur bones for a living. This work is entirely honorable and I, for one, enjoy watching the television documentaries that result from these expeditions. However, there will be no demand for such services during the war, and not for some time afterward, not until some measure of social stability and prosperity are reestablished.

However, there will be continuing demand for basic skills in the more primitive wartime economy. You should avoid occupations for which no real wartime equivalent exists. Those who dig up dinosaur bones in peace time will have only their skill at shoveling earth to fall back on during the hostilities. Automobile mechanics and electricians possess skills for which there will be wartime demand. Electrical engineers and automobile designers, for example, will likely experience difficulty as many large scale enterprises are shut down or scaled back. Unlike dinosaur diggers, however, these individuals have skills that will enable them to find work as electricians and automobile mechanics.

Those employed by the government will experience a variety of economic fates. Consider, for example, the case of an anglo lady working for the department of social services of some Arizona county that borders Mexico. This area will revert to Mexico. This person's job will either no longer exist, or will be given to an hispanic. Consider also that the new county government will not pay her pension if she manages to retire before the fighting starts. Avoid working for local or state governments that will be run by those not of your tribe after the war. Be aware now that your pension will not be paid if you are a retiree. If not retired prior to hostilities, you will no longer have a job. Assuming you are able to escape with your life, you will have to start from scratch in a new area.

Federal employees, if white, will do better, but others will face a different set of difficulties. Consider, for example, the case of a black person employed as a senior manager with the federal Department of Transportation. The new white, northern government will not keep him at his job. In fact, its troops will most likely shoot him on sight. His job and pension with the federal government will be lost. The government of the new black, southern nation will be in such economic difficulty that it is unlikely he will continue to be a civil servant. If he does find work with the new government of the new black nation, his new salary will be a fraction of his former one.

On the whole, highly skilled self-employment in some basic occupation seems the best bet.

Paper financial assets such as cash and bonds will take a hellish beating. The classic pattern in war is that actual physical goods available for purchase diminish, while the paper available to purchase them with increases. That means severe inflation. Stocks, being claims on real physical assets, should in theory do better, but keep in mind that all locatable assets will be directly or indirectly subject to confiscation by the government. Paper assets may be confiscated by paper—taxation or inflation. Physical assets will be seized physically.

Be advised that in addition to hostiles not of your tribe, armed members of your own tribe—including the new government—will take your property in ways that are now considered theft. Secondly, be advised that what the government (and other armed bands) can't locate, they can't steal or tax or confiscate. You should structure your physically assets accordingly.

I recommend that you avoid overly expensive vehicles. To armed soldiers, brand new, loaded, 4WD vehicles tend to look more militarily desirable than used, stripped-down pickup trucks. And if they are drunk, Porches will look like military vehicles as well. And remember, they have the guns.

To cover every aspect impacting your survival during Civil War II is either beyond the scope of this book or is simply impossible for anyone excepting yourself to calculate. Your well-being during the war is your burden. If you haven't realized that, then I have thus far failed you.

Imperial America is on it knees dying. This fact, as an individual, you can not really change, Therefore, to prepare yourself and your family for Civil War II, you must first change yourself. When you read the newspapers, listen to the news on TV and notice events as you go about your everyday life, pause and consider these unfolding events from the Civil War II perspective. Ask yourself if they indicate that this nation is still on course for Civil War II. Ask yourself how these events will impact you, your livelihood, and your local area five, ten, and twenty years from now.

Once you develop this habit of examining events from the Civil War II perspective, you will see more clearly the dangerous trends in our society that converge in Civil War II, and that these trends are both accelerating and mutually reinforcing. Do not delude yourself into thinking that the government will correct these dangerous trends prior to their getting completely out of hand. Once you have the proper overall attitude for survival in Civil War II, then you can address the specifics of survival. As an old soldier, I wish you good luck, and bid you keep your head down.

Civil War II Checklist

"It would indeed be the ultimate tragedy if the history of the human race proved to be nothing more noble than the story of an ape playing with a box of matches on a petrol dump."—David Ormsby-Gore

Let's summarize some of the key factors which will measure our march toward Civil War II. Concerned individuals are invited to watch for their development. The events of this checklist are in no particular order of importance or sequence of occurrence. Some have already occurred to some degree, but should be monitored for further growth.

Item 1: If the racial tattooing of ethnic classifications on ID cards and other documents persists, we'll know the countdown clock is ticking. Every time you see a blank for your ethnic group on a form, think Civil War II.

Item 2: If illegal aliens are allowed to vote, even in local elections, it will be another unmistakable signal that American citizenship, and therefore America itself, is finished. If the millions of illegal aliens in America are granted amnesty and get the vote, it will mean open immigration and a giant step towards Civil War II.

Item 3: The abolition of the right to bear arms. This must be done to reduce the military potential of those assigned to the bottom tier of the emerging multiethnic American Empire. Those in higher tiers will retain their guns—and thereby their military resources—through devices such as the Nation of Islam's security company and street gangs. Imperial conversion cannot be completed without breaking the military potential of the white working class, the historic key to military dominance of North America. In colonial times, the arrogant British imperial establishment mistakenly thought the key to the military dominance of North America consisted of imperial European armies and alliances with Indian tribes. Ordinary, native born, white Americans and their militias were treated with sneering scorn, good only for a hearty laugh before being brushed aside by His Majesty's imperial redcoats. If the current imperial establishment has any sense of history, they will not repeat George the Third's folly.

Item 4: Watch for racially split juries.[1] If jurors begin to refuse to convict their co-ethnics, then our progress towards basic social breakdown and Civil War II is accelerating. This will be one of the most serious indicators that we're edging closer to a social earthquake and a breakup along tribal fault lines. Some prominent blacks have already encouraged black jurors to consider jury nullification. In a short piece in Harper's magazine, Paul Butler, a black lawyer, said this about the hypothetical case of a black drug addict whom black jurors know to be guilty of burglary of a "rich white family":

> "For example, if the offense was committed to support a drug habit, I think there is a moral case to be made for nullification, at least until such time as access to drug-rehabilitation services are available to all."[2]

Watch for states to allow conviction by a majority of a jury. Currently, only Louisiana and Oregon allow conviction by majority, but the Supreme Court ruled in 1972 that even a 9 to 3 majority is constitutionally sufficient for

---

1 *The New York Times*, "Two Trials Reflect City's Two Worlds", March 24, 1992, p. 12.
2 *Harper's Magazine,* December, 1995, adapted from Paul Butler's article "Racially Based Jury Nullification: Black Power in the Criminal Justice System" in the *Yale Law Journal.*

conviction. Eventually, the Supreme Court will suspend the right to trail by jury altogether in the final stages of imperial conversion.

Item 5: Watch for the military to assume police duties. Empires must of necessity use terror and brute force to suppress their lower tiers and masses of poor people. Because local police departments often lack the appropriate resources, empires often employ regular military units in this role.

Brazil's military often conducts sweeps through its slums where they liberally dispense beatings, torture and summary executions. The Brazilian Army officers say they're fighting the drug traffickers, but as one cynical slum dweller pointed out, if they really wanted to kill the drug Mafia godfathers they could easily do so because everybody in Brazil knows exactly who they are and exactly where they live in Brazil's luxurious walled suburbs. When you think about it, doesn't that sound a lot like our drug situation here?

Look for the national guard or the regular military to assume police duties in our cities. In Puerto Rico, the national guard is already on permanent patrol in housing projects,[3] and this role for the national guard has been suggested for Washington D.C. and Boston.[4] Also, watch for police stations and military bases to be hardened to end their current vulnerability to siege as described in a previous chapter. Also watch for retired military officers to assume high government posts, especially in areas of law enforcement, especially drug law enforcement, both foreign and domestic. This will promote the militarization and brutalization of our police, and the politicians can line up behind this phony "War on Drugs." Also, watch for military-type assaults on urban gangs in the name of

---

3 *The New York Times*, July 23, 1995, p. 22.
4 *The New York Times*, October 27, 1993, p. 2.

fighting the drug menace. The real target will be the gangs themselves and their military power.

I say that just as Columbia is a narco-state, and just as Mexico is in the final stage of conversion into a narco-state, our own United States of America is itself in the initial stages of transformation into a narco-state.

Item 6: Watch for the establishment of an elite military force outside the chain of command of the regular military to serve as an internal counterinsurgency force. The Russians have exactly such a military force called Internal Security which is under the command of the interior ministry (the MVD), not the regular military. The MVD internal security has its own tanks, helicopters and artillery and its primary mission is suppressing internal disturbances too serious for the police such as mutinies of regular military units, riots, strikes by workers, and ethnic rebellions such as the recent uprising in Chechnya.[5] One tactic of the MVD Internal Security is using troops of one ethnic group to put down civilian rebellions of other ethnic groups. The same principle of control was used by the British in the days of their empire, when they employed German mercenaries during our revolution, and when they used Sikhs from India to control the Chinese population of Singapore. One of our existing federal formations, most likely the BATF, will evolve into our MVD-type internal security, acquiring heavier and heavier weapons and military organizational structure.

Item 7: Watch for Washington D.C. to increasingly resemble the capitol of some banana republic under siege by revolutionaries and mobs. Specifically, watch for riots in Washington D.C. to grow in scope until they menace the White House and the Congress. Ultimately, federal military units will have to be permanently stationed there to

---

5 Andrew Cockburn, *The Threat*, Random House, 1983, p. 48.

protect our government from its own citizens. In May, 1995, truck bomb barriers were installed in front of the White House,[6] yet another indication that our government is under siege from its own citizens.

Item 8: Resegregation: Watch for Africans and other minorities demanding, and often getting, separate facilities for themselves, another clear sign that they're continuing to reject co-option.

Item 9: Watch for further replacement of individual rights by group rights, group rights based on ethnic group. Empires employ this method to enlist certain favored groups in suppressing the others, and racist affirmative action is a classic example of this replacement of our rights as individuals by a race-based system of penalties and special privileges. Then the powers that be have only to pay off the leaders of these favored groups, a relatively easy task. Every time you hear the racist euphemism affirmative action, think Civil War II.

Item 10: Watch for non-governmental organizations acquiring military power. As we are increasingly losing our common identity as Americans, people are increasingly turning to alternate sources of psychological fulfillment and the increasingly necessary military protection that such organizations are extending. The Waco cult, street gangs, the Nation of Islam, and white militias are all partly manifestations of this trend. Some of these groups will be militarily crushed by the government, while others will be tolerated or even subsidized as their assigned tier in the multiethnic American Empire dictates.

The recent tragedy in Waco was an example of the crush, and the granting of 20 million dollars in security guard contracts by the Department of Housing and Urban Development to the Nation of Islam[7] is an example of the

---

6 *The New York Times*, May 21, 1995, p. 1.
7 *The New York Post*, March 24, 1995. Ed Koch column in Editorial

subsidize side of this policy. The Washington establishment knew full well that any attempt to disarm the powerful Muslim militia would provoke massive rioting and firefights in every major American city. Instead, the establishment is paying protection money to the disciplined Muslim militia to keep the lid on the ghettos in an act of appeasement that is sure to backfire in the long run. Every time you hear of a non-governmental organization acquiring military power, think Civil War II.

Item 11: Watch for real political power to continue to shift from our elected officials to the courts, and thus away from the American people. Since the Sixties, the real power of the judicial branch of our government has been vastly expanded at the expense of the legislative and executive branches. This is no accident. Recall that judges are almost always appointed, often for life. The people have no effective way of ridding themselves of these usurpers of our Bill of Rights. These unelected judges use euphemisms like affirmative action to promote imperial tiering while they summarily strip citizens of their traditional and constitutional rights.

The recent invalidating of many provisions of California's proposition 187,[8] the anti-illegal alien measure, is an illustration of how the federal judiciary blocked the democratically expressed will of the people when it threatened a key provision of the imperial agenda—the deliberate flooding of America with illegal aliens to break labor unions, lower wages, and transform America into a third-world country.

This steady usurpation of power by the judicial branch is the means by which the American branch of the international elites is transforming America into a third-world country manipulated by an oligarchy. All reforms inter-

---

Section.
8 *The New York Times*, November 21, 1995, p. 10.

fering with the internationalist elitist agenda have been and will continue to be struck down as "unconstitutional" by the Supreme Court. Unless the American people retake our judicial system, Civil War II is unavoidable.

Item 12: Watch for more instances of real political power flowing from American institutions to international bodies, thus again flowing away from American citizens. Specifically, watch for NAFTA-type treaties that hand over to international bodies the power to regulate matters concerning American trade, taxes and control of our borders. Since World War II, real financial power has increasingly flowed to foreign and multinational corporations. National laws that restrict the international flow of goods and people also restrict the profits of these transnational corporations. Because these multinationals are increasingly acquiring all the financial power, they will continue to acquire the real political power that money always brings, and they will do so by the simple bribery of our corrupt politicians with the usual PAC money.

One recent manifestation of this power is the replacement of literally tens of thousands of American workers by foreigners working for less, whom the multinationals recruit and import into America on H-1B nonimmigrant visas.[9] In my home state of New Jersey, computer programmers from India were imported and replaced American programmers who were fired as soon as they trained these Indian replacements. If the multinationals can't move the factory to a foreign country, then they move the foreign workers to America. Either way Americans lose jobs and the multinationals get richer, and thus acquire yet more power.

---

9 *Morris County New Jersey Daily Record*, Nov. 27, 1994, p. 1; *The New York Times*, Sept.7, 1995.

Every time you hear NAFTA, the IMF, the World Court, or the UN, think New World Order and think Civil War II.

Item 13: Watch for minorities and radical whites to continue to seize control of American institutions. Our courts, schools, universities, the media, many churches, and many unions have been completely or partially taken over, and politically incorrect dissidents expelled or intimidated into silence.

Item 14: Watch for secessionist movements and other movements seeking autonomy on American soil. Some of these movements will be subsidized by corporations seeking territory free from American law and taxes where they may plunder to their hearts' content. The so-called Pequot Indian reservation in Connecticut is a recent example of this actual carving up of America.[10] A foreign corporation, an unidentified Malaysian corporation, financed this sham reservation. These sham Indians don't even have to identify this foreign corporation, or pay any federal, state or local taxes because they are legally a sovereign nation. Nor are they subject to American Law, yet our courts have allowed them to annex American land adjacent to theirs.

Many of these Pequot Indians look like they just got off a 747 from Jamaica while others have blonde hair and blue eyes. Don't let that fool you though. These are real, genuine, bona fide, authentic Indians because our imperial legal system decreed them such.

This sorry episode is a graphic example of how America is actually being geographically fragmented and carved up right now, today, under our very noses. A foreign corporation was able to set up an independent nation on American soil because the establishment is so

---

10 *The New York Times*, April 26, 1994, Sect. B, p. 1; May 22, 1994, p. 1; May 2, 1995, Sect. B, p. 4; May 4, 1995, Sect. B, p. 5.

corrupt that it's selling slices of America as if it were a pizza. And how are these mock Indians able to sustain their fraud? Why by the simple bribery of our corrupt officials, of course, and shame on you if you didn't think of it. These imitation Indians are now the fifth largest contributor to the Democratic National Committee.

Item 15: Watch for race-based political parties, a sure sign of racial polarization. The most telling statistic occurred when ex Ku Klux Klansman David Duke ran for governor of Louisiana and got a majority of the white vote, an estimated 55%.[11] The establishment media hailed his defeat as a rejection of race-based politics by American voters, but actually the exact opposite was the case. The white citizens of Louisiana are clearly fed up with being forced to ride in the back of the liberal establishment's affirmative action bus deporting them to the multiethnic empire, and are inclined towards Civil War II right now, today. In time, most working-class white Americas will likewise be forced to join them. Watch for black-based and Hispanic-based political parties to emerge, or for an avowedly leftist or rightist or any third party to achieve major party status. Also watch for the Republican party to become the *de facto* white, populist, and rightist party; and for the Democratic party to become the radical leftist and minority party.

In 1994, Georgia had 10 representatives in the federal house of Representatives—eight white Democrats, one black Democrat and one white Republican. Then Georgia was allocated another seat to reflect a population increase. Currently the Georgia delegation figures are eight white Republicans and three black Democrats.[12] Currently, there are no black Republicans or white Democrats in the Georgia delegation. This stunning, overnight reversal was

11 *The New York Times*, October 8, 1990, p. 1.
12 *The New York Times*, April 28, 1995, p. 8; August 15, 1995, p. 12.

produced by redistricting designed to maximize the number of black representatives. However, regardless of the technical manner by which it is brought about, the racial polarization of our political parties will proceed throughout the south and across the nation. In 1965 there were 90 white congressional Democrats from the 11 states of the old Confederacy, in 1985 there were 72, in 1995 there were 42. In 1965 there were 16 white congressional Republicans from the 11 states of the old Confederacy, in 1985 there were 43, in 1995 there were 66.[13] This shift to a white Republican south represents a complete and stunning reversal of a stable system that had been firmly in place since our first civil war. Things are beginning to boil down in Dixie.

As our two major parties increasingly become radicalized and racialized, our government will oscillate from left to right with increasing violence as these two parties alternate in office. Eventually these increased oscillations will cause our country to topple into Civil War II.

Item 16: Watch for the emergence of "no-go" areas for the police in our cities, areas abandoned by the police and left to the control of street gangs. The existence of these areas will be officially denied of course, and the police will occasionally mount media oriented forays into them, but it will be pure theater.

Item 17: Watch for a so-called slave tax refund or some similar vehicle that will automatically subsidize all blacks for life.[14]

Item 18: Watch for court orders and other schemes mandating more voting districts in which blacks are intentionally a majority. This was one of the reasons for the graphic racial breakdown of the Georgia congressional delegation mentioned earlier.

---

13 *The New York Times*, July 23, 1995, p. 16.
14 *The New York Times*, July 21, 1994, Sect. B, p. 10.

Item 19: Watch other multiethnic empires for ethnic violence, a general loss of democracy, increasing poverty, waves of refugees, and their actual breakup in ethnic warfare. South Africa, Russia, Turkey, the Balkan countries, Brazil, all of black Africa, Mexico, Guatemala, India, Pakistan and Peru are all multiethnic empires to some extent. As they go, so will America. Every time you see ethnic warfare in some foreign multiethnic country, ask yourself if we're not becoming more and more like them every day. If you think we are, then think Civil War II.

Item 20: Watch for the spread of walled suburbs, euphemistically labeled as gated communities. America is taking on the appearance of medieval Europe, and for exactly the same reasons—marauding criminals, marauding gangs of criminals and, eventually, marauding armies of criminals. Approximately four million Americans now live in communities literally encircled by walls and security guards. Most are affluent whites who will increasingly vote against municipal improvements because they feel safe against the turmoil outside their gates and walls.

Where is this concept taking us? Why in the general direction of Brazil, of course. An article in the May 14, 1994 issue of *The New York Times* was titled: "A City of Blondes Build Walls: Migrants Keep Out" The *Times'* article described how the affluent Brazilian city of Blumenau with many people of German descent had gone to great lengths to keep out poor and unemployed Brazilians. The city officials had even put out tourist brochures containing this cheery message: "Get to know this tropical Germany. Enjoy blue-eyed, blond-haired Brazilian hospitality." Is this the sort of future we want for America—walled cities of affluent blue-eyed blonds encircled by shanty towns of a brown and black underclass?[15] These walled suburbs are manifestations of the racial, economic, psychological and geographic fragmentation of America, and will hasten their ultimate manifestation in Civil War II.

Item 21: Watch for more mind control hoaxes by the establishment media. The establishment media still employs one exposed hoaxer whose favorite deception is announcing that she is broadcasting live from some location while she is in fact inside a closed sound studio posing in front of a picture of that location. This trickster has even been known to wear winter clothing while posing in front of one of her fake facades located inside a perfectly warm studio when it's cold at the location she is supposedly broadcasting from.[16]

Some establishment newspapers like New York's *Newsday* merge two separate photographs together.[17] This trick is commonly used to make people appear as if they were together when they were actually in different places. Time Magazine retouches photographs of people to make them look more or less menacing as their spin doctors fancy.[18] NBC employs hoaxers who use explosions to create hoaxes, while other NBC hoaxers use fake photographs to accuse people of wrongdoing.[19] All of these were deliberate, premeditated hoaxes, but in only one instance were any of these hoaxers dismissed by these establishment news organizations.

As Civil War II approaches, the establishment media, in conjunction with the political establishment, will increase its manufacture of mindcontrol hoaxes to accuse politically incorrect persons of wrongdoing so that the

---

15 *The Washington Post*, April 9, 1994, Sect. E, p. 1; *The New York Times*, May 4, 1994, p. 4; May 3, 1994, Sect. B, p. 1.
16 *The New York Times*, Feb. 17, 1994, Sect. D. p.22.
17 *Ibid.*
18 *The New York Times*, June 21, 1994, p. 22; June 25, 1994, p. 8.
19 *Time Magazine*, "When Reporters Break the Rules", March 15, 1993, p. 54.

government can intimidate them, harass them, send them to prison, and even assassinate them. Likewise, hoaxes will be used to cover up wrongdoing so that those favored by the establishment can escape public censure, and deserved legal punishments. Every time you hear slanted news from the establishment media, think Civil War II.

Item 22: Watch for an increasing percentage of minorities in our military, the use of foreigners in our military, the use of UN troops on our soil, or even the establishment of an American Foreign Legion. Recall that empires often employ foreign mercenaries to put down internal rebellions, just as the British employed German mercenaries to crush our War of Independence, because citizen soldiers are often reluctant to fire upon their fellow citizens or co-ethnics.

In the May 1, 1995 issue of Time magazine, Gen. John Sheehan of the United States Marine Corps was quoted as saying that Cubans interned in refugee camps in Guantanamo Bay, Cuba should be recruited into the American Military.[20] Such foreign mercenaries (and that's exactly what they would be) would have far less qualms about firing on American citizens than American soldiers would.

General Sheehan was also quoted as saying that enlisting the Cubans would be cheaper than enlisting Americans. This stated reason is both a reason and a pretext. It is a reason because it would in fact save money as desperate foreign mercenaries would work for less, thus allowing the military to lower its pay levels, driving out Americans, especially white Americans. It is a pretext because foreigners would be ideal for Waco-type operations because they wouldn't jeopardize their livelihood by refusing orders. That's a big, big attraction for our

---

20 *Time Magazine*, May 1, 1995, p. 21.

establishment, so watch for foreign mercenaries being inducted into the US military.

Also, watch for minorities in our military in excess of their percentage in the total population. The United States Army is now 40% minority. If this trend continues, by 2050 AD the United States Army will be 80% minority. Will a minority *coup d'etat* be far behind when for every white soldier there are 2 black and 2 Hispanics soldiers?

Item 23: Watch for more out of court settlements in cases of alleged racial discrimination. As mentioned earlier, one tool of imperial governments is hiring certain groups to oppress others. Institutions captured by radicals, like our universities, are now transferring large sums of tax money directly to radical groups without the consent of the people by out of court settlements. This bypasses our elected representatives and whatever remaining protection our courts might provide us.

Our government should forbid out of court settlements in cases of alleged racial discrimination when tax money is demanded as part of the settlement. But of course our corrupt politicians won't, so watch for more funding of black racist and radical groups by out of court settlements as our corrupt universities and corrupt politicians pave the road to Civil War II with the people's tax money.

Item 24: Watch for more restrictions on freedom of speech by the government and the establishment media. This will drive non-establishment people underground and radicalize them. All manner of radical underground newsletters and other media will appear, which will give the government an excuse for yet more unconstitutional means of silencing them by harassment by the FCC, and other more direct—even terminal—means, by the BATF and the FBI. Every time you hear of someone being fired, or otherwise punished for some politically incorrect utterance, think Civil War II.

Item 25: Watch for police to increasingly abandon their traditional uniforms for ones that resemble military and secret police uniforms in their dark color or camouflage, military helmets, opaque face shields, and absence of name tags. These costumes are meant to intimidate, as are the tactics of using paid perjurers (known as informers), paid liars (known as expert witnesses), wiretaps, boots kicking in doors, agent provocateurs, attack dogs, tanks, gas, and entrapment followed by assassination by sniper.

These measures are meant to intimidate not only the people they're taking out, but more importantly those who view these Roman circuses on TV so they'll be fearful to speak up in defense of the victims. Also, these Robo Cop costumes have a profound impact on those who don them. Dress a man like a stormtrooper and he'll soon enough get the message.

Our police should wear only light blue, their traditional color, the traditional color of liberty. Their faces should be visible at all times, and they should have large nametags visible at a distance. They should be forbidden to conduct nighttime raids except to rescue hostages, or when human life is clearly and immediately threatened. They should be forbidden the use of armored vehicles and gas in all circumstances. And they should be forbidden the use of entrapment except in cases of persons previously convicted of felonies.

Most establishment types scoff at assertions that America is evolving into a police state. But here's what former governor of South Dakota, Joe Foss, said as quoted in the May 5, 1995 issue of the *New York Post.*[21]

"Call a spade a spade. That's always been my philosophy. As a result of (the) Oklahoma City (bombing) (President Clinton) wants a lot more restrictions on things. I call that heading towards a police state."

---

21 *The New York Post*, May 5, 1995, p. 8.

These operations like the Waco takeout and against the Weavers are looking more and more like Vietnam-style Search and Destroy operations and Vietnam-style Phoenix assassination teams.

Item 26: Watch for clandestine groups of white officers to form within our federal, state and local police—groups similar to the Resisters in the Green Berets. I predict that these white law enforcement resister groups will be clandestine because those openly holding such opinions are being harassed and/or fired by higher ups to enforce unconstitutional, racist affirmative action programs and to politicize our law enforcement agencies.

These white law enforcement Resisters will forewarn the victims of unconstitutional actions such as raids for guns or entrapments that target people like Randy Weaver solely because they have antiestablishment views.

These white law enforcement Resisters will destroy evidence intended to convict white citizens accused of violating the racist and unconstitutional affirmative action laws. Regrettably, as conditions become extreme, white law enforcement Resisters will also destroy evidence intended to convict whites of crimes against blacks.

The white law enforcement Resisters will be forced to take these measures because they are fed up with being victims of racist affirmative action purges themselves, and because they have a duty to their conscience and to our constitution to fight racism, and because they are coming to realize that by enforcing these racist affirmative action laws that they are delivering up their own children to a racist Moloch of a society that will treat whites as neo-slaves with no rights that blacks need respect.

With a quarter for an anonymous phone call or evidence quickly dropped into a garbage can, these white law enforcement Resisters will effectively strike back at racist affirmative action programs and assaults on our Bill of Rights. White law enforcement and military personnel will begin to flash the World War II "V" for victory sign to indicate that they are part of the resistance. I predict that flashing of the "V" for victory sign will spread to white civilians.

The appearance of Resisters in our law enforcement agencies will be another sure sign that Civil War II draws nearer. Actually, white law enforcement Resisters may be organizing right now. The "Washington Whispers" section of the May 22, 1995 issue of *US News and World Report* had a mention of one such possible resister unit. It said that an anonymous memo had been circulating among white officers of the Drug Enforcement Agency. The memo was titled: *A catalogue of insidious abuses of affirmative action within the DEA.*[22]

The memo pointed out that minority agents were being promoted despite indiscretions that had prevented the advancement of white agents. DEA Chief Thomas Constatine denounced the memo as "vicious and divisive," and said those responsible would be dealt with "swiftly and stringently." Apparently, Mr. Constatine is totally unfamiliar with the First Article of our Bill of Rights, a seeming requirement for federal law enforcement officers these days. Chief Constatine should be dealt with.

Item 27: Watch for an arm of the federal government charged with promoting racist affirmative action, such as the Equal Employment Opportunity Commission, to acquire agents that carry guns and have the power to make arrests.

Item 28: Watch for the collapse of the US dollar as the world's premier currency. This will be the signal that will confirm our status as a third-world nation. Foreigners (notably, the Japanese) will refuse to continue to buy our federal government debt instruments denominated in US

---

22 US News and World Report, May 22, 1995, p. 25.

dollars. Currently, we enjoy the ability to borrow US dollars and repay in US dollars. Because inflation and devaluation are constantly eroding the value of the American dollar, foreigners are increasingly being paid back in a currency (dare we say, funny money) that has lost much of its real value. Eventually, they will demand that our federal government issue debt instruments denominated in (and repayable only in) their own currency. Our government will have no choice but to comply, and this will signal that we are in the same category as any other third-world country, however much the establishment denies it.

Item 29: Watch for growing geographic segregation and its increasing mention in the establishment press. One such article was the previously mentioned *New York Times* article of Aug. 20, 1995: "Immigrants in, native whites out."[23] Another, also previously mentioned, occurred in the July 17, 1995 issue of *Newsweek* about whites fleeing California for the Rocky Mountain states: "It got so it was nothing but Bloods, Crips, drug addicts and wetbacks."[24]

Item 30: Watch for signs that the global military equation and American dominance in it are being challenged. One such sure sign would be the acquisition of a blue-water navy by the Japanese. Japan cannot be a global military power without a blue-water navy, and Japan cannot have a serious blue-water navy without aircraft carriers. Should Japan acquire even one aircraft carrier, it will mark a direct challenge to American dominance, however much it is denied by Washington and Tokyo. The same applies to a Japanese alliance with China or Russia. Unfortunately, one recurrent theme of history is that trade wars usually escalate into shooting ones. Also, watch for the breakup of NATO, or the emergence of some military

---

23 *The New York Times Magazine*, August 20, 1995, p. 44.
24 *Newsweek*, "The West at War", July 17, 1995, p. 26.

arrangement in Europe that in any way displaces NATO. In the future, unlike the recent past, any foreign power or alliance in opposition to America will have the option of assisting ethnic groups in America to the point of armed rebellion. Expect them to play this card.

Item 31: Watch for the breakup of Canada. If Canada does break up along ethnic and linguistic lines, it will bode ill for its neighbor which is an even worse multiethnic and multilingual mishmash.

Item 32: Watch for an increased flow of Americans immigrating to Canada. In 1991, 13,500 Canadians immigrated to America, but only 5,270 Americans immigrated to Canada.[25] Should this trend ever reverse itself, and more Americans immigrate to Canada than Canadians immigrate to America, then we shall know that America is becoming increasingly untenable for white Americans.

Item 33: Watch for political and legal organizations formed along ethnic lines that will parallel, and ultimately displace their official rivals. For instance, watch for organizations with names like The Association of Hispanic States, or the Black Mayors Conference.

Item 34: Watch for more help wanted ads stating that job applicants must be bilingual. In the southwest, many advertisements for jobs such as nurses and salespeople specify that the applicant must be bilingual. This will tend to accelerate the flight of Anglos out of the southwest and hasten Civil War II. Every time you see a help wanted ad requiring bilingualism, think Civil War II.

Item 35: Watch for indications that the UN is assuming the role of a world government, and that the US is losing even more of its national sovereignty to the UN. Occupation of the United States by United Nations troops is not the fantasy of militia groups that the establishment press

---

25 *Statistical Abstract of the US*, 1994, p. 11; *Canada Year Book*, 1994, p. 116.

makes it out to be. Consider that it is not entirely clear that member nations may withdraw from the United Nations. Recall our first civil war. Attempted peaceful secession by the southern states was answered by an armed invasion and occupation by armies of the northern states even though there was nothing in the Constitution that explicitly forbade secession by member states. Now we find ourselves in a parallel situation with the United Nations. Because (to the best of my knowledge) nothing in the UN Charter expressly allows a nation to withdraw, any attempt by the United States to quit the United Nations may be used as grounds for an invasion by UN troops.

Those who scoff at such an invasion have plainly not considered the future from the Civil War II perspective. Consider an America locked in all-out civil war, her once huge fleet scuttled by mutineers or divided into clashing fragments. Hispanic secessionists controlling the southwest might invite in UN "peace keeping" troops in hopes of thereby getting some form of international recognition. The legitimate government in Washington might object and quit the UN. Japan or other foreign powers could coerce the other nations into sanctioning this UN invasion with the intent of delivering a fatal blow to the already crippled America, the last step into turning America into a Japanese vasal state chiefly useful for farming. (There is a joke circulating among Japanese businessmen: America is a farm, Europe a boutique.) Note that the Hawaiian secessionists have based their claims for independence in part on a United Nations resolution, Resolution 1514, which deals with "decolonization." Watch for the Hawaiians and other secessionists to make more appeals to the UN in the future, such as requesting and getting permission to speak before the UN, and even being granted representation in certain UN committees, or UN affiliated bodies.

Watch for calls for the formation of a permanent military force directly under the command of the UN. Should the UN acquire such a force, there can be no doubt but that the international establishment has decided that the UN will be converted to an actual world government dominate over its member countries. This final step should be regarded as inevitable because the UN is an ideal vehicle for the international establishment to control every last nation, institution and person on Earth. This is the case because the voting members of the UN are not representatives elected by the people, but "ambassadors" appointed by heads of state, and thus at least one step removed from the people.

Item 36: Watch for a certain picture. We've all seen this picture countless times before, a picture from Beirut, Budapest, Afghanistan, Vietnam, Sri Lanka, Yugoslavia, Somalia—a burnt-out tank, perhaps the charred corpse of a crewman protruding through a hatch, and jubilant rebels posing atop the tank waving assault rifles and a flag. Someday we shall see this picture in our newspapers yet again, and this time taken on American soil. The tank, the dead crewman, and rebels will all be Americans. All will be American except the flag, which will be a Mexican, Aztlan, New Africa, or Confederate flag. When we see this picture, it will be too late. Civil War II will be upon us. But there's another picture we'll see first, again one we've all seen before from some unfortunate land. But this time it will be taken right here in the US of A—a picture of a dirty, ragged child foraging for food in a garbage dump. You shutter bugs out there, note that the first to get this picture published in a magazine or newspaper will probably get a Pulitzer Prize.

This item concludes the Civil War II checklist. This checklist is intended to encourage you to consider these and other current events from the Civil War II perspective. The unfortunate events that daily parade past on our TV screens and front pages are not unrelated and random things. They have a common underlying cause, and all draw lines that converge on a single focal point in the future. The underlying cause is the transformation of America into an undemocratic, multiethnic, third-world empire, and the common outcome they all point at is Civil War II.

As you go about your everyday affairs, I invite you to consider unfolding events from the Civil War II perspective. Ask yourself if these events fit into a larger pattern. Do they indicate that Civil War II is drawing nearer or receding? Ask yourself what causes the political and media establishments are assigning to these events. Does the establishment's perspective really explain unfolding events, or merely shift blame away from themselves? Are they attempting to shift the blame to irresistible historic forces supposedly beyond their control, such as assigning closed factories to restructuring for the information age? Is the establishment blaming some event on the lowest tier of the emerging empire—working-class whites—by calling them racists? Is the establishment using their explanation of some recent event as a pretext to grant special privileges to some tier of the empire in exchange for their support, such as setting aside scholarships, or jobs, or contracts for some minority group? Think for yourself, and decide for yourself.

The End of America and Western Civilization

All the world waits to see if America will become a multiethnic, democratic nation with a nonracial social contract, or if it will devolve into an ethnically and socially-tiered third-world empire, and shatter exactly as all other multiethnic, undemocratic empires have throughout world history. When America erupts in flames, all the world will rightly conclude that Liberty's torch set her ablaze, and that democracy and a multiethnic society are mutually exclusive.

Western Civilization will be transformed; tribalism will blossom into its ultimate expression. Nations will unite into super blocks of Europeans against Africans, Christians against Moslems, East against West, and rich against poor until some hideous climax predator claws its way to the top of the smoking global bone heap. And what excuse will we Americans have? That our fathers didn't leave us a Bill of Rights to light our way? That no one cautioned us that a house divided against itself cannot stand? That no one told us that we should judge one another by character rather than color?

Like all men of goodwill, I ask nothing more than to live peacefully in my own country where I enjoy the equal protection of the law without corruption of blood, exactly as set down in our Constitution. Regrettably, this simple and just concept is dead, and so is America.

Quotes

I will leave you with a box of military and philosophical chocolates to sample and pass judgement on at your leisure. Help yourself, or as we used to say in 'Nam—knock yourself out. . . .

Men rise from one ambition to another—first they seek to secure themselves from attack, and then they attack others. —Machiavelli

Governments need armies to protect them from their enslaved and oppressed subjects.—Tolstoy

Whoever has an army has power, and war decides everything. —Mao Tse-tung

Great empires are not maintained by timidity.—Tacitus

Ultima ratio regnum (The final argument of Kings)—Inscribed on French cannon by order of King Louis XIV

Still, if you will not fight for the right when you can easily win without bloodshed; if you will not fight when your victory will be sure and not too costly; you may come to the moment when you will have to fight with all the odds against you and only a precarious chance of survival. There may even be a worse case. You may have to fight when there is no hope of victory, because it is better to perish than live as slaves.—Winston Churchill

They (the Athenians) have an abundance of gold and silver, and these make war, like other things, go smoothly.—Hermocrates of Syracuse

When princes think more of luxury than of arms, they lose their state.—Machiavelli

If historical experience teaches us anything about revolutionary guerrilla war, it is that military measures alone will not suffice. —USMC Gen. Samuel Griffith

. . . make them so sick of war that generations would pass away before they would again appeal to it.—Union Gen. William T. Sherman on conducting the war of aggression against the Confederacy

We must act with vindictive earnestness against the Sioux, even to their extermination, men, women, and children. Nothing less will reach the root of the

cause.—Gen. William T. Sherman on conducting war of agression against the Indians

Better a dog in time of peace than a man in time of war.—Chinese Proverb

The great questions of the day will be decided not by speeches and majority votes . . . but by blood and iron.—Bismark

The instinctive need to be the member of a closely-knit group fighting for common ideals may grow so strong that it becomes inessential what these ideals are.—Konrad Lorenz

And it's one, two, three what are we fighting for? Don't ask me I don't give a damn; next stop is Vietnam.—Country Joe McDonald and the Fish

In war more than anywhere else in the world things happen differently from what we had expected, and look differently when near from what they did at a distance.—Karl von Clausewitz

War involves in its progress such a train of unforeseen and un-supposed circumstances that no human wisdom can calculate the end. It has but one thing certain, and that is to increase taxes.—Thomas Paine

There is many a boy here today who looks on war as all glory, but boys, it is all hell.—Gen. William T. Sherman

The greatest pleasure is to vanquish your enemies and chase them before you, to rob them of their wealth and see those dear to them bathed in tears, to ride their horses and clasp to your bosom their wives and daughters.—Genghis Khan

I want no prisoners. I wish you to burn and kill. The more you burn and kill, the better it will please me.—Gen. Jacob Smith during the "pacification" of the Philippines

It is better to die on your feet than live on your knees.—Emiliano Zapata, Mexican revolutionary

There is no human affair which stands so constantly and so generally in close connection with chance as war.—Karl von Clausewitz

In one sense the charge that I did not fight fair is true. I fought for success and not for display. There was no man in the Confederate army who had less of the spirit of knight errantry in him, or who took a more practical view of war than I did.—John S. Mosby, Confederate guerilla leader.

There is one source, O Athenians, of all your defeats. It is that your citizens have ceased to be soldiers.—Demosthenes

War gives the right to the conquerors to impose any conditions they please upon the vanquished.—Julius Caesar

Nothing can seem foul to those that win.—Shakespeare, in *King Henry IV*

Never, never, never believe any war will be smooth and easy.—Winston Churchill

Duty is ours, consequences are God's.—Stonewall Jackson

Waste 'em all and let God sort 'em out.—Vietnam helmet graffiti

In the midst of peace, war is looked on as an eventuality too distant to merit consideration.—Vegetius

In the final choice, the soldier's pack is not so heavy a burden as a prisoners chains.—Eisenhower

The logical end of a war of creeds is the final destruction of one.—Lawrence of Arabia

And you know that peace can only be won when we've blown 'em all to kingdom come.—Country Joe McDonald and the Fish

It is better to have no son than one who is a soldier.—Chinese proverb

Victory at all costs, victory in spite of all terror, victory however long and hard the road may be; for without victory there is no survival.—Winston Churchill

War loses a great deal of its romance after a soldier has seen his first battle.—John S. Mosby, Confederate guerrilla leader

A great war always creates more scoundrels than it kills.—Unknown

He who makes war his profession cannot be otherwise than vicious. War makes thieves, and peace brings them to the gallows.—Machiavelli

A great war leaves a country with three armies—an army of cripples, and army of mourners, and an army of thieves.—German proverb

After 'Nam, everything was just a stone bore.—Anonymous Vietnam vet

What you will see here is the price of freedom.—Sign over the entrance of a Veterans Administration hospital

If the war didn't kill you, it was bound to start you thinking.—George Orwell

Peace is an armistice in a war that is continuously going on.—Thucydides

We had to destroy the village in order to save it.—An American Army officer in Vietnam

It is not merely cruelty that leads men to love war, it is excitement.—Henry Ward Beecher

I discovered to my amazement that average men and women were delighted at the prospect of war. I had fondly imagined what most pacifists contended, that wars were forced upon a reluctant population by despotic and Machiavellian governments.—Betrand Russell

The spectacle of a spontaneous rising of a nation is rarely seen. though there be in it something grand and noble which commands our admiration, the consequences are so terrible that for the sake of humanity, we ought to hope never to see it.—Jomini, French military theorist

For it is not profusion of riches or excess of luxury that can influence our enemies to court or respect us. This can only be effected by fear of our arms.—Vegetius

Let them hate us so long as they fear us.—Caligula, Roman Emperor

The ugly truth is revealed that fear is the foundation of obedience.—Winston Churchill

Wars spring from unseen and generally insignificant causes, the first outbreak being often but an explosion of anger.—Thucydides

The urge to gain release from tension by action is a precipitating cause of war.—Liddell Hart, British military historian and theorist

Eternal peace is a dream, and not even a beautiful one. War is part of God's world order. In it are developed the noblest virtues of man: courage and abnegation, dutifulness and self-sacrifice. Without war the world would sink into materialism.—Helmuth von Moltke, World War I chateau general

War is sweet to those who have never experienced it.—Pindar

Those who do not go to war roar like lions.—Kurdish saying

An opinion can be argued with, a conviction is best shot.—Lawrence of Arabia

If you want peace, understand war.—Liddell Hart

The first virtue in a soldier is endurance of fatigue; courage is only the second virtue.—Napoleon

Those who make peaceful revolution impossible will make violent revolution inevitable.—John F. Kennedy

A revolution is not a bed of roses. A revolution is a struggle to the death between the future and the past.—Fidel Castro

Among other evils which being unarmed brings you it causes you to be despised.—Machiavelli

An empire founded by war has to maintain itself by war.—Montesquieu

If we must be enemies, let us be men, and fight it out as we propose to do, and not deal in hypocritical appeals to God and humanity.—Union Gen. William T. Sherman to Confederate Gen. John B. Hood

History is littered with wars which everybody knew would never happen.—Enoch Powell, British Parliamentarian

Thomas W. Chittum was a rifleman in the United States Army in Vietnam in 1965 and 1966, a rifleman in the Rhodesian Territorials in the early Seventies, and a rifleman in the Croatian Army in 1991 and 1992. He was a computer programmer for most of his adult life. He is now a writer and lives in rural New Jersey.

Mr. Chittum writes a weekly column that examines current events from the Civl War II perspective. Representatives of publications interested in his column are invited to contact him. He is available as a radio and television talk show guest. You may contact him at PO Box 6235, Parsippany, NJ 07054, or through his World Wide Web page at http://members.aol.com/chittum/cw2index.html.

For a free catalog of other interesting books, write to:
American Eagle Publications, Inc.
P. O. Box 1507
Show Low, AZ 85901
or call (800)719-4957 today!